Narrative *of the* Residence
of
Fatalla Sayeghir
among the
Wandering Arabs
of the
Great Desert

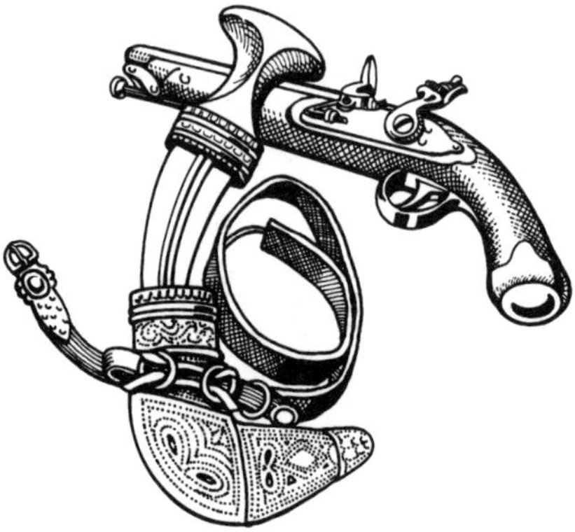

THE FOLIOS ARCHIVE LIBRARY

NARRATIVE *of the* RESIDENCE *of* FATALLA SAYEGHIR *among the* WANDERING ARABS *of the* GREAT DESERT

COLLECTED AND TRANSLATED BY
M. DE LAMARTINE

ORIGINAL EDITION PUBLISHED BY
CAREY, LEA & BLANCHARD
PHILADELPHIA, 1836

Garnet
PUBLISHING

NARRATIVE OF THE RESIDENCE OF FATALLA SAYEGHIR

Published by
Garnet Publishing Limited
8 Southern Court
South Street
Reading
RG1 4QS, UK

This edition copyright © Garnet Publishing, 1996

All rights reserved
No part of this book may be reproduced in any form or by any
electronic or mechanical means, including information storage and
retrieval systems, without permission in writing from the publisher,
except by a reviewer who may quote brief passages in a review

New edition

ISBN 1 85964 088 5

British Library Cataloguing-in-Publication Data
A catalogue record for this book is available from the British Library

Jacket design by David Rose
Illustrations by Nick Williams

Printed by Bookcraft (Bath) Limited

Contents

Introduction by Robert Irwin	vii
Note on Production	xvi
Introduction by Alphonse de Lamartine	A2
Narrative of Fatalla Sayeghir	13
List of Tribes	204

Introduction

On 1 July 1798 a French expeditionary force, sent by the Directorate and under the command of General Napoleon Bonaparte, landed in Egypt. A decree printed in Arabic and French was distributed to those Egyptians who were prepared to receive it. It denounced the Mamluk elite who governed Egypt in the name of the Ottoman Sultan: 'For too many years that gang of slaves purchased in Georgia and the Caucasus has tyrannised over the most beautiful region of the world. But God the almighty who rules the universe has decreed that their rule shall come to an end'. The aims of the expedition were various, though somewhat vague. In part, the Directorate hoped to protect and extend French commercial interests in the Levant. Egypt and Syria were important customers for French textiles and other products. At the same time those lands supplied France with rice, wheat and cotton. The occupation of Egypt would, it was thought, strengthen France's hold on the Mediterranean. It would also allow the French to clear the British from the Red Sea and even to threaten British possessions in India. (With this in mind, a team of savants who had accompanied the army to Egypt carefully considered the practicability of digging a Suez Canal.)

Whatever the Directorate's aims, Bonaparte himself had grander ideas. He envisaged himself as a second Alexander and fantasised about moving out of Egypt to occupy Syria and from there marching east through Iraq and Persia to conquer India. Alternatively, he could advance on Constantinople and, having conquered the capital and heartlands of the Ottoman Empire, march through the Balkans and Germany back to France. Things went well at first. Even before landing in Egypt, Bonaparte's army had captured Malta from the Knights of Malta. In Egypt, the

French defeated the Mamluk Beys in a succession of pitched battles and then went on to invade Palestine. However, the Mamluks, who retreated into Upper Egypt, continued to fight a guerrilla war. In Palestine, Ahmad Jezzar Pasha and Sidney Smith successfully defended the port of Acre against the French. Plague spread through Bonaparte's army. But the greatest disaster of all took place at sea. On 1 August Nelson's fleet sank most of the French ships at the so-called 'Battle of the Nile'. At a stroke the French enterprise became hopeless, for the expeditionary force no longer enjoyed secure communications with France nor could it be supplied or reinforced. In August 1799 Bonaparte slipped away back to France and by 1801 the remnants of the French occupying force were shipped back to France – humiliatingly on British ships.

The whole thing had been an unqualified disaster. But this did not stop the Emperor Napoleon, as Bonaparte eventually became, continuing to dream of a French empire in Asia. Although Napoleon and his marshals concentrated their energies on the conquest of Europe, a series of French agents were sent to the Near East to survey the routes and make contacts with local rulers. Jaubert was sent to Persia and in 1810 Colonel Boutin was despatched to Iraq to investigate the possibility of using Basra as a port of embarkation for India. He landed in Alexandria in 1811 and took the guise of a commercial agent, but was murdered by predatory Bedouins in 1815.

Such missions of reconnaissance were finally rendered pointless by the disasters suffered by French armies, first in Russia in 1812 and later at Waterloo in 1815. However, French ambitions to occupy, or at least establish some sort of protectorate over large parts of the Ottoman Empire did not die with Bonaparte. Nineteenth-century politicians and polemicists argued that it was France's duty to do so. That duty was arrogantly presented as a *mission civilisatrice*. Chateaubriand described Bonaparte's expedition as 'a ray

Introduction

of light cast into the shadows of Islam and a breach made in barbarism'. It was argued that the leading role played by the French in the Crusading expeditions and the defence of the Crusader states in the twelfth and thirteenth centuries conferred special responsibilities on France in that region. The Christian Maronites in Lebanon deserved the protection of Catholic France. Above all, most thoughtful observers concluded that the Ottoman Empire could not hold together for much longer and many of them argued that France, invariably at odds with Britain and fearful of Russian ambitions to occupy Constantinople, should not be left out of the inevitable scramble for the territories of the disintegrating Turkish Empire.

Alphonse de Lamartine (1790–1869) was to become one of the most influential advocates for an active French role in the Near East. Lamartine was one of the leading French poets of the nineteenth century. He achieved early fame with the Romantic *Méditations poétiques* (1820) and his reputation was confirmed with a second anthology of poems, *Harmonies poétiques et religieuses* (1830). The latter poems are pervaded by the poet's metaphysical preoccupations and show the ill-digested results of Lamartine's readings in Hinduism and in the mystical ideas of the Martinist movement. After the publication of *Harmonies*, Lamartine attempted to go into politics. He was at first unsuccessful and, in the wake of his defeat at an election, he set out for the Middle East. He and his wife and daughter settled in Beirut at first and from there he made journeys through the rest of Lebanon and into northern Syria and Palestine. A pilgrimage to Jerusalem was the culmination of his travels. Lamartine wanted to journey through the lands where the events of the Bible had taken place while looking for a suitable landscape to frame his own religious and metaphysical musings.

More generally, he must have expected to find literary inspiration in the exotic Arab lands. He may have hoped to repeat the success of Chateaubriand's *Itinéraire de Paris à Jerusalem* (1811). In the event, his trip resulted in the publication of *Souvenirs, Impressions, Pensées et Paysages Pendant un Voyage en Orient, 1832–1833 ou Notes d'un Voyageur* (1835). This was a fragmentary account of his travels interspersed with his poems as well as with meditations on the Turks, the Arabs, Christianity, poetry, the soul and the cosmos. Lamartine was not much taken with the Bedouin. He regarded them as ignoble savages, though he did become an enthusiast for an Arab popular epic which celebrated the exploits of the pre-Islamic Bedouin hero, Antar. *Voyage en Orient* also included a description of an encounter with the eccentric, ageing adventuress, Lady Hester Stanhope. Lamartine was disconcerted not to find himself recognised as a great poet, but he nevertheless described her in a fulsomely romantic fashion.

When the *Voyage en Orient* was first published, its (already considerable) bulk was swollen by all sorts of supporting material, including the exceedingly curious *Narrative of the Residence of Fatalla Sayeghir among the wandering Arabs of the Great Desert*. The manuscript of this work had apparently been procured for Lamartine by his interpreter, Mazolier, whom Lamartine had taken into service when he was in Beirut. Mazolier procured the work following a discussion in the region of Tiberias, during which Lamartine had expressed some interest in the way of life of the Arabs of the Syrian desert. Fatalla's Arabic text had been translated into French of a sort by Mazolier, Lamartine then improved on the French, as well as correcting a few blatant errors. Fatalla was a Christian Arab interpreter who came from Aleppo. According to the story he tells, he was taken on by a Bonapartist secret agent, Theodore Lascaris, in 1810, and together they went out into the Syrian desert. Their mission, which was a little vague, was to investigate a possible route to India, to recruit tribes sympathetic to the French interest and to create a great Bedouin confederacy. In the

INTRODUCTION

end many of their hopes were pinned on the 'Drahy' – who can be very tentatively identified as al-Dra'i ibn Sha'lan, Sheikh of the Ruwala Bedouins. Fatalla presents a vivid account of Bedouin life, the more interesting in that it comes from the pen of an urban Arab.

However, the main value of Fatalla's narrative would seem to be in its detailed account of the Wahhabi warriors, their raids into Syria, their religious beliefs and the policies of their leaders, as well as Lascaris's attempts to create a Syrian tribal confederacy opposed to the Wahhabis under the leadership of the 'Drahy'.

In the early eighteenth century, Muhammad ibn 'Abd al-Wahhab preached a revivalist, fundamentalist version of Islam. He and his followers wished to revert to those practices which were enjoined by the Qur'an or sanctioned by the practice of the Prophet Muhammad and his contemporaries. Since they wished to purify Islam of all later excrescences, they were opposed to Arab cultic practices and folk medicine. They were hostile to the cult of saints and the veneration of tombs. They rigorously enforced the prayers and the month of fasting and they declared an absolute ban on tobacco, music, dancing and silken clothes. Even the minaret was deemed to be an undesirable innovation. Abd al-Wahhab and his descendants formed an alliance with a Najdi tribal leader, Muhammad ibn Saud, and, after the latter's death the partnership continued with Ibn Saud's descendants. In 1806 the Wahhabi warriors, led by Saud ibn'Abd al-'Aziz, occupied Mecca and during the first decade of the nineteenth century, they made a series of damaging raids into Iraq and Syria. Their ideological fervour and military successes seemed to threaten the hold of the Ottoman Turks on the Arab provinces.

Lascaris, we learn from Fatalla's narrative, played a leading role in organising the resistance of the Syrian desert tribes to the Wahhabi menace. At the end of Fatalla's story, Lascaris's scheming and squandering of money among the people of the desert are seen to come to nothing, for Bonaparte's retreat from Moscow, and French losses endured during that retreat had destroyed any prospects of a future French expedition to Syria.

Fatalla's narrative is a unique and curious document. The story is vivid and exciting, but it is too exciting to be true. The book is a fraud. The boldness of Fatalla's imposture can be compared to George Psalmanazar's wholly imaginary account of life in eighteenth-century Formosa, or to the no less fanciful account of life in the East Indies given by Princess Caraboo (later unmasked as Mrs Neale from Bristol). It is true that Theodore Lascaris did actually exist. He was one of a small handful of Knights of Malta who took service with Bonaparte after the French occupation of the island. In Egypt during the French Occupation, Lascaris occupied a series of administrative posts of modest importance. He liaised closely with the pro-French Coptic Legion and became an advocate of their potential importance. He married a Georgian slave girl, Sitt Mariam. He also fell in love with the Arab lands and learnt Arabic. This was his golden time, but after the French withdrawal from Egypt, he failed to find any secure or dignified employment in France, or later in Smyrna. Eventually, he fetched up as a stateless person in northern Syria. Though he was always full of grand projects for promoting French (or sometimes British) strategic and commercial interests in the East, he at first earned a living by teaching music and writing in Aleppo. Subsequently, he abandoned this and went to live in the village of Nebk where he and his obese wife subsisted at a miserable level by selling cloth and various gewgaws to the Bedouin of the Syria desert. From the accounts of others who met him, he emerges as a querulous and rather pitiful figure who was forever building castles in the clouds. He was not a dashing Bonapartist agent. Hester Stanhope met Lascaris and kept him briefly in her retinue. (When she came to read Lamartine's book, she was horrified by

Introduction

Lamartine's romanticised and inaccurate account of herself, but she was sarcastically entertained by Fatalla's nonsense.)

It is impossible to think that Fatalla's account of Lascaris, the master spy and adventurer, was written in good faith. There are too many inconsistencies and errors in his story for one to treat him as merely Lascaris's dupe. Fatalla's work is a fiction, which just occasionally draws on the facts for inspiration. So he really should be regarded as one of the earliest Arab novelists. It would be interesting to know more about him. As it is, one cannot even be sure that his real name was Fatalla, or, for that matter, that the narrative of 'Fatalla' was not written by Mazolier, in order to get money from Lamartine.

The Arabic manuscript of Fatalla's work is to be found in the Bibliothèque Nationale in Paris, *fonds arabe*, MS no. 2298. Fatalla also seems to have written in 1843 an account of the occupation of Syria by Ibrahim Pasha and the manuscript of this is also in the Bibliothèque. In an afterword to a later edition of *Voyage en Orient*, published in 1875, Lamartine gave an account of how one day in 1847 Fatalla, or at least an old Arab claiming to be Fatalla, turned up on his doorstep in Paris. Fatalla brought Lamartine up to date with more fanciful stories about the 'Drahy', the Wahhabis and Arab life. Lamartine, enthralled and grateful, arranged for Fatalla to be sent back to Syria at the expense of the French government and to be rewarded for his services to France. Thereafter, the literary impostor vanished into obscurity.

Information about the Wahhabis and about the life of the Arabs of the Syrian desert was hard to come by in the early nineteenth century. The travels of Jean Louis Burkhardt and of Ulrich Seetzen were less well-known than they should have been. Fatalla's imposture went undetected for several decades and parts of his story were recycled in serious histories of the region. Then the Arabist Fulgence Fresnel in Egypt translated a key chapter of the narrative back into Arabic and had a pious religious scholar who had formerly advised the Wahhabi leader, Saud, comment on Fatalla's account of the meeting at Dariyya between Saud and the Drahy. Ahmad al-Hanbali's report was damning. The supposed meeting had never taken place. Saud was described as tanned when he was pale. Dariyya was not so much described as fantasised about by someone who had never been there. In large matters and small ones Fatalla's account was utterly false. The chapter translated into Arabic by Fresnel together with its damning commentary is also in the Bibliothèque Nationale, *fonds arabe* MS no. 2999.

That Fatalla's narrative is a work of fiction makes it more, rather than less interesting. It plays upon the vogue in the eighteenth and nineteenth centuries for noble-savage romances about the desert life. The romance of *Antar* was translated and adapted throughout Europe and Rimsky-Korsakov's music is probably the most enduring legacy of this mania. Eyles Irwin's *The Bedouins, or Arabs of the Desert* (1802), an opera which was successfully performed in Dublin, is one example of the many expressions of the nineteenth-century enthusiasm for wild Arab ways. While there is no agreement as to which was the first novel written in Arabic, the origins of the Arabic novel are conventionally sought in the late nineteenth century. Fatalla's fiction predates the earliest candidates by several decades. True, it pretended to be non-fiction, but then so did Daniel Defoe's *Journal of the Plague Year* (1722) and that has claims to be the first English novel. At another level, Fatalla's story was well-pitched to appeal politically to those who, like Lamartine, continued to entertain Napoleonic dreams of a French Empire in the Orient.

After his return from Syria, Lamartine enjoyed considerable success as a politician and he became a strong advocate of France taking a protective role regarding the Maronites. The Ottoman Empire had more life in it than predatory European observers had thought and it was not

INTRODUCTION

until the end of the First World War that France was able to secure protectorates in Syria and Lebanon.

ROBERT IRWIN

Note on Production of this Edition

This book has been photographed from the original first edition. The quality of the type as reproduced on the pages therefore reflects the printing technology available at that time. A slight distortion of the type has also occurred during the photographic process, but this should not impair the reading of the text. We feel that the benefits of capturing the original style of the book and its period out-weigh the disadvantages of any minor distortions to the type.

INTRODUCTION.

BY ALPHONSE DE LAMARTINE.

We were encamped in the midst of the desert which extends from Tiberias to Nazareth, and were speaking of the Arab tribes we had met in the day, of their manners, and the connexions between them and with the great population by whom they are surrounded. We endeavoured to elucidate the mystery of their origin, their destiny, and that astonishing endurance of the spirit of race, which separates this people from all other human families, and keeps them, like the Jews, not without the pale of civilization, but within a civilization of their own, as unchangeable as granite.

The more I have travelled, the more I am convinced that races of men form the great secret of history and manners. Man is not so capable of education as philosophers imagine. The influence of governments and laws has less power, radically, than is supposed, over the manners and instincts of any people, while the primitive constitution and the blood of the race have always their influence, and manifest themselves, thousands of years afterwards, in the physical formations and moral habits of a particular family or tribe. Human nature flows in rivers and streams into the vast ocean of humanity: but its waters mingle but slowly, sometimes never; and it emerges again, like the Rhone from the Lake of Geneva, with its own taste and colour. Here is indeed an abyss of thought and meditation, and at the same time a grand secret for legislators. As long as they keep the spirit of race in view, they succeed; but they fail when they strive against this natural predisposition: nature is stronger than they are. This sentiment is not that of the philosophers of the present time, but it is evident to the traveller; and there is more philosophy to be found in a caravan journey of a hundred leagues, than in ten years' reading and meditation. I felt happy in thus wandering about among deserts and unknown countries, with no route before me but my caprice; and I told my friends, and M. Mazolier, my interpreter, that if I were alone and without family ties, I would lead this manner of life for years and years. I would never sleep where I had arisen; I would transport my tent from the shores of Egypt to the Persian Gulf, and wish no aim for the evening but evening itself. I would wander on foot, and dwell with eye and heart on these unknown lands, these races of men so different from my own, and contemplate humanity, this most beautiful work of God, under all its forms. To effect this, what would be requisite? —a few slaves or faithful servants, arms, a little gold, two or three tents, and some camels. The sky of these countries is almost always warm and pure, life easy and economical, and hospitality certain and picturesque. I should prefer, a hundred times, years passed under different skies, with hosts and friends ever new, to the barren and noisy monotony of the life of our capitals. It is undoubtedly more difficult to lead the life of a man of the world in Paris or London, than to visit the universe as a traveller. The results of two such lives are, however, very different. The traveller either dies, or he returns with a treasure of thoughts and wisdom. The domesticated inhabitant of our capitals grows old without knowledge, without experience, and dies as much entrammelled, as much immersed in false notions, as when he first begins to exercise his senses. I should like, said I to my dragoman, to cross those mountains, to descend into the great desert of Syria, accost some of the large unknown tribes that traverse it, receive their hospitality for months, pass on to others, study their resemblances and differences, follow them from the gardens of Damascus to the banks of the Euphrates and the confines of Persia, and raise the veil which still hangs over the civilization of the desert,— a civilization where our chivalry had its birth, and where it must still exist: but time presses, and we may see but the borders of that ocean whose whole no one has yet crossed. No traveller has penetrated amidst those innumerable tribes, whose tents and flocks cover the plains of the patriarchs; one only man attempted it, but he is no more, and the notes which he had collected during ten years' residence amongst the people were lost with himself. I desired to introduce M. de Lascaris to my readers: the following is a sketch of his character.

M. de Lascaris was born in Piedmont, of one of those Greek families which settled in Italy after the conquest of Constantinople: he was a knight of Malta when Napoleon conquered the island. M. de Lascaris was then a very young man; he followed him to Egypt, attached himself to his fortunes, and was fascinated by his genius. Highly gifted himself, he was one of the first to perceive the lofty eminence reserved by Providence for the young man who was imbued with all the spirit of Plutarch, when the human character seemed worn out, shattered, or false. He perceived more: he perceived that the great work to be accomplished by his hero was not perhaps the restoration of power in Europe; an effect which the reaction of men's minds rendered necessary, and therefore easy; he felt that Asia presented a far wider field for the renovating ambition of a hero; that that was the scene for conquering, for founding, and for renovating on a scale incomparably more gigantic; that despotism, brief in Europe, would be lasting, eternal, in Asia; that the great man who could there apply the principles of organization and unity would effect more than Alexander,—more than Bonaparte in France. It appears that the young warrior of Italy, whose imagination was luminous as the East, undefined as the desert, wide as the world, held some confidential conversations with M. de Lascaris on this subject; and directed one ray of thought towards that horizon which was opening to him his destiny. It was but a ray, and I lament it:

it is evident that Bonaparte was the man for the East, not the man for Europe. This will provoke a smile; it will appear paradoxical to the world. But consult travellers. Bonaparte, who is looked upon as the man of the French revolution and of liberty, never understood liberty, and wrecked the French revolution. History will prove it in every page, when written under other impulses than those which at present dictate it. He was the incarnation of reaction against the liberty of Europe: glorious and brilliant, it is true; but no more. What proof shall I advance? Ask what remains of Bonaparte in the world, beyond a page of warfare, and a page to record an unskilful restoration. But as for a monument, a basis for expectation, a future, a something that may live after him besides his name—nothing exists but an immense reminiscence. In Asia he would have stirred men by millions; and, himself a man of simple ideas, he would with two or three facts have built up a monument of civilization which would have survived him a thousand years. But the mistake was made: Napoleon chose Europe; he only chose to leave behind him one explorer to examine what might be done, and to trace out the road to India, if ever fortune should lay it open to him. M. de Lascaris was the man; he set out with secret instructions from Bonaparte, received the necessary sums for his undertaking, and established himself at Aleppo, to complete his knowledge of Arabic. Being a man of merit, talent, and knowledge, he feigned a sort of enthusiasm to account for his continuance in Syria, and his unceasing intercourse with the Arabs of the desert who came to Aleppo. At length, after some years' preparation, he commenced his grand and perilous enterprise; he passed with various risks, and under different disguises, through all the tribes of Mesopotamia and of the Euphrates; and returned to Aleppo, rich in the knowledge he had acquired, and in the political relations he had prepared for Napoleon. But whilst accomplishing the mission, fortune overthrew his hero; and he learned his downfall the very day on which he was about to bring him the fruits of seven years' danger and devotion. This unforeseen stroke was fatal to M. de Lascaris; he went into Egypt, and died at Cairo, alone, unknown, abandoned, and leaving behind him his notes, his only bequest. It is said that the English consul obtained these valuable documents, which might have become injurious to his government, and that they were either destroyed or sent to London.

"What a pity," said I to M. Mazolier, "that we should have lost the result of so many years' labour and patience!" "There is something yet remaining," said he; "I was attached at Latakia, my country, to a young Arab, who accompanied M. de Lascaris during all his travels. After his death, being without resources, and deprived even of the arrears of his small salary, which M. de Lascaris had promised him, he returned poor and plundered to his mother. He is now living in some small employ with a merchant of Latakia. I knew him there, and he has often spoken to me of a series of notes that he wrote at the instigation of his patron in the course of their wandering life." "Do you think," said I to M. Mazolier, "the young man would consent to sell them?" "I should think so," he replied; "and the more so, as he has often expressed his desire to present them to the French government. But nothing is so easy as to know this; I will write to Fatalla Sayeghir, which is the name of the young Arab. Ibrahim Pacha's Tartar will deliver him my letter, and we shall have an answer on his return to Said." "I commission you," said I, "to negotiate the affair, and to offer him two thousand piastres for his manuscript."

Some months elapsed before the answer of Fatalla Sayeghir reached me. Returning to Byrauth, I sent my interpreter to negotiate directly for the MS. at Latakia. The terms were accepted, the sum was paid, and the Arabic MS. brought me by M. Mazolier. In the course of the winter, I got them translated with infinite difficulty into the Frank language, and thence translated them into French myself; the public are thus enabled to enjoy the fruits of a ten years' journeying, which no other traveller has hitherto effected. The extreme difficulty of this triple translation must be an excuse for the style of the notes. The style indeed is of little importance in such works; facts and manners are every thing. I am fully satisfied that the first translator has altered nothing; he has only suppressed some tedious details consisting of idle repetitions which availed nothing.

Should this recital possess any interest in a scientific, a geographical, or a political point of view, I have only one wish to form; it is that the French government, which such a period of peril and exile was intended to enlighten and serve, should show a tardy gratitude towards the unfortunate Fatalla Sayeghir, whose services might even still be useful. In this wish I include too the young and skilful interpreter, M. Mazolier, who has translated these notes from the Arabic, and who accompanied me for a year in my travels in Syria, Galilee, and Arabia. Versed in the knowledge of Arabic, the son of an Arab mother, nephew of one of the most powerful and revered sheiks of Lebanon, having already traversed all those countries with me, familiar with the manners of the tribes, a man of courage, intelligence and honour, heartily devoted to France, this young man might be of the utmost service to the government in our relations with Syria. French nationality terminates not with our frontiers. Our country has sons as attached upon shores whose name she scarcely knows. M. Mazolier is one of those sons. France should not forget him. No one could serve her better than he, in countries in which the effects of our activity of civilization, protection, and even of policy, must soon be necessarily felt. The following is the narrative of Fatalla Sayeghir, literally translated.

NARRATIVE

OF

FATALLA SAYEGHIR.

At eighteen years of age I quitted Aleppo, my country, with a stock of merchandise, to establish myself in Cyprus. Being tolerably fortunate in the first year of my commercial speculations, I took a liking to the business, and adopted the fatal idea of taking to Trieste a cargo of the productions of the island. In a short time my goods were embarked; they consisted of cotton, silk, wine, sponge, and colocynth. On the 18th March, 1809, my ship, commanded by Captain *Chefalinati*, set sail. I was already calculating the profits of my venture, and rejoicing at the idea of the gross returns, when, in the midst of my delightful illusions, the fatal news arrived of the capture of the vessel by an English ship of war, which had taken her to Malta. In consequence of such a loss, I was obliged to strike my balance, and retire from trade; and I quitted Cyprus totally ruined, and returned to Aleppo. Some days after my arrival I dined at one of my friends' with several persons, amongst whom was a stranger, very ill-dressed, but to whom much consideration was shown. After dinner there was music; and the stranger sitting beside me, conversed with much affability: we spoke of music, and after a long conversation, I rose to ask him his name. I learned that it was M. Lascaris de Ventimiglia, and that he was a knight of Malta. The following day, I saw him coming to my house, holding in his hand a violin. "My good young man," said he on entering, " I remarked yesterday how much you like music; I already look upon you as my son, and bring you a violin, of which I beg your acceptance." I received with much pleasure the instrument, which was exactly to my taste, and gave him very many thanks. After an animated conversation of two hours, during which he questioned me upon all sorts of subjects, he retired. The next day he returned, and continued in this manner his visits for a fortnight; he then proposed to me to give him lessons in Arabic for an hour every day, for which he offered me a hundred piastres a month. I gladly accepted this advantageous proposal; and after six months' teaching he began to read and speak Arabic tolerably well. One day he said to me, "My dear son, (he always addressed me thus,) I see that you have a great inclination for commerce; and as I wish to remain some time with you, I should like to employ you in a manner agreeable to yourself. Here is money: purchase goods, such as are saleable at Homs, at Hama, and the neighbourhood. We will trade in the countries least frequented by merchants; you will find we shall succeed well." My desire of remaining with M. de Lascaris, and the persuasion that the undertaking would be successful, determined me to accept the proposal without hesitation; and I began, according to a note which he sent me, to make the purchases, which consisted of the following articles: red cloth, amber, corals in chaplets, cotton handkerchiefs, silk handkerchiefs black and red, black shirts, pins, needles, box combs and horn, rings, horses' bits, bracelets of glass beads, and other glass ornaments; to these we added chemical products, spices, and drugs. M. Lascaris paid for these different articles eleven thousand piastres, or two thousand tallaris.

The people of Aleppo, who saw me purchasing the goods, told me that M. Lascaris was become mad. Indeed his dress and his manners made him pass for mad. He wore his beard long and ill-combed, a white turban very dirty, a shabby robe or *gombaz*, with a vest beneath, a leather belt, and red shoes without stockings. When spoken to, he pretended not to understand what was said. He spent the greater part of the day at the coffee-house, and ate at the bazaar, which was never done by the higher people. This behaviour had an object, as I afterwards discovered; but those who knew it not thought his mind was deranged. As to myself, I found him full of sense and wisdom; in short, a superior man. One day when all the goods were packed, he called me to him, to ask what was said of him at Aleppo. " They say," replied I, " that you are mad." " And what do you think yourself?" said he. " I think that you are full of sense and knowledge." "I hope in time to prove it so," said he; "but I must have you engage to do all I shall order, without reply or asking a reason; to obey me in every thing; in short, I must have a blind obedience; you will have no occasion to repent." He then told me to fetch him some mercury; I instantly obeyed: he mixed it with grease and two other drugs, of which I was ignorant, and assured me, that a thread of cotton dipped in this preparation and tied round the neck was a security against the bite of insects. I thought to myself there were not insects enough at Homs, or at Hama, to require such a preservative; that therefore it was destined for some other country; but as he had interdicted every remark, I merely asked him on what day we should depart, that I might order the moukres (camel drivers.) "I allow you," he replied, "thirty days to divert yourself; my chest is at your disposal; enjoy yourself, spend what you like, spare nothing." This is, thought I, for a farewell to the world which he wishes me to make: but the strong attachment I already felt for him stifled this reflection; I thought no longer but of the present, and availed myself of the time he allowed to enjoy myself. But alas! the time for pleasure soon passes! it soon came to an end. M. Lascaris pressed me to depart; I submitted to his orders, and profiting by a caravan that set out for Hama, Thursday the 18th of February, 1810, we left Aleppo, and arrived at the village of Saarmin, after twelve hours' march. The next day we set out for Nuarat el Nahaman, a pretty little town, distant six hours. It is celebrated for the salubrity of the air and the goodness of its waters; it is the native place of the celebrated Arabian poet Abu el Hella el Maari, who was blind from his birth. He had learned to write by a singular method. He remained in a vapour bath while they traced on his back the form of the Arabic letters with iced water. Many are the traits of sagacity related of him; among others the following:—Being at Bagdad with a calife, to whom he was continually boasting of the air and water of his native place, the calife procured some water from the river Nuarat, and without any intimation gave it him to drink. The poet, immediately recognising it, exclaimed, "Here is its limpid water, but where its air so pure!" To return to the caravan: it remained two days at Nuarat, to be present at a fair that was held there on Sundays. We went to walk about, and in the multitude I lost sight of M. Lascaris, who had disappeared in the midst. After looking for him a long while, I at last discovered him in a solitary spot conversing with a ragged Bedouin. I asked him with surprise what pleasure he found in the conversation of such a person, who could neither understand his Arabic, nor make him understand his. "The day," said he, "when I have first had the honour of speaking with a Bedouin, is one of the happiest days of my life." "In that case," I replied, "you will often be at the summit of happiness, for we shall be continually meeting with this sort of people."

He made me buy some *galettes* (the bread of

the country) and some cheese, and gave them to Hettall, (the name of the Arab,) who thanked us and took leave. The 20th February we left Nuarat el Nahaman, and, after six hours' march, we arrived at Khrau Cheikhria, and the next day, after nine hours, at Hama, a considerable town, where we were known to nobody, as M. Lascaris had brought no letters of recommendation. We passed the first night in a coffee-house; and, the next day, hired a room in the khan of Asshad Pacha. As I was beginning to open the bales, and prepare the goods for sale, M. Lascaris said to me with a dissatisfied air, "You are only thinking of your miserable commerce! If you knew how many more useful and interesting things there are to be done!" After that I thought no more of selling, and went to survey the town. On the fourth day, M. Lascaris, walking by himself, proceeded as far as the castle, which is falling to ruins. Having examined it attentively, he had the imprudence to begin taking its dimensions. Four vagabonds, who were concealed under a broken arch, threw themselves upon him with threats to denounce him for wishing to carry off treasures, and introduce the giaours into the castle. With a little money all might have been ended without noise; but M. Lascaris defended himself, and with difficulty escaped from their hands and came to me. He had not finished telling me his adventure, when we saw two men from the government enter with one of the informers. They took the key of our room, and led us away, driving us with sticks like felons. Being brought into the presence of the mutzelim, Selim Beg, known for his cruelty, he thus questioned us: "Of what country are you?" "My companion is from Cyprus," I replied, "and myself from Aleppo." "What object leads you to this country?" "We are come to trade." "You lie; your companion was seen about the castle, taking its dimensions and drawing plans; it is to obtain treasure, and deliver the place to the infidels." Then turning to the guards, "Take the two dogs," said he, "to the dungeon."— We were not allowed to say another word. Being brought to the prison, we were loaded with chains from the neck to the feet, and shut up in a dark dungeon, which was so small that we could hardly turn. After a time we obtained a light, and some bread, for a tallari; but the immense quantity of bugs and other insects that infested the prison prevented us from closing our eyes. We had scarcely courage to think of means to get out of the horrible place. At length I recollected a Christian writer, named Selim, whom I knew by reputation as a useful person. I gained over one of our guards, who went for him; and the following day Selim arranged the matter by means of a present of sixty tallaris to the mutzelim, and fifty piastres to his people. At this price we obtained our liberty. This imprisonment procured for us the acquaintance of Selim, and several other persons at Hama, with whom we passed three weeks very agreeably.

The town is charming; the Orontes crosses it, and renders it gay and animated; its abundant waters keep up the verdure of numerous gardens. The inhabitants are amiable, lively, and witty. They admire poetry and cultivate it with success. They have been well characterised with the epithet of speaking birds. M. Lascaris having asked Selim for a letter of recommendation to a man of humble condition at Homs, who might serve us as guide, he wrote the following note: "To our brother Yakoub, health! They who will present you this letter are pedlers, and come to you to sell their wares in the neighbourhood of Homs; assist them as far as you are able. Your pains will not be lost; they are honest people. Farewell!"

M. Lascaris, well satisfied with this letter, wished to take advantage of a caravan that was going to Homs. We departed on the 25th March, and arrived after six hours at Rastain, which is at present only the ruin of an ancient considerable town. It contains nothing remarkable. We continued our route, and at the end of another six hours we reached Homs. Yakoub, to whom we delivered our letter, received us admirably, and gave us a supper. His trade was making black cloaks, called machlas. After supper, some men of his own rank came to pass the evening with him, drinking coffee and smoking. One of them, a locksmith named Naufal, appeared very intelligent. He spoke to us of the Bedouins, of their manner of living and making war; he told us that he passed six months of the year with these tribes to arrange their arms, and that he had many friends among them. When we were alone, M. Lascaris said to me that he had that night seen all his relatives; and as I expressed my wonder at learning that there were any of the people of Ventimiglia at Homs, "My meeting with Naufal," said he, "is more valuable to me than that with my whole family."

It was late when we retired, and the master of the house gave a mattress and covering for us both. M. Lascaris had never slept with any one; but, out of kindness, he insisted that I should share the bed with him: not wishing to contradict him, I placed myself beside him; but as soon as the light was out, wrapping myself in my machlas, I crept out to the ground, where I passed the night. The next morning, on waking, we found ourselves lying in the same manner; M. Lascaris having done as I had. He came and embraced me, saying, "It is a good sign that we had the same idea, my dear son; for I like to call you so, as it pleases you, I hope, as well as me." I thanked him for the interest he showed me, and we went out together to prevail on Naufal to accompany us through the town, and show us what curiosity it contained, promising to pay him for the loss of the day. The population of Homs is about eight thousand. The character of the people is quite different from that of the inhabitants of Hama. The citadel, situated in the centre of the town, is falling to ruins; the ramparts still preserved are watered by a branch of the Orontes. The air is pure. We bought for forty piastres two sheep-skin cloaks like those of the Bedouins: these cloaks are water-proof. To be the more at liberty, we hired a room at the khan, and begged Naufal to stay with us, engaging to pay him as much as he would have earned in his shop,—about three piastres a day. He was of the greatest use. M. Lascaris questioned him dexterously, and obtained from him all the information he wished: getting him to describe the manners, usages, and character of the Bedouins, their mode of receiving strangers and treating them. We stayed thirty days at Homs, to wait the return of the Bedouins, who commonly quit the neighbourhood of that city in October, to proceed to the south, according to the weather, and the water and pasturage; progressing one day, and halting five or six. Some go as far as Bagdad, others to Chatt el Arab, where the Tigris and the Euphrates join. In February they commence their return to Syria, and at the end of April they are found again in the deserts of Damascus and Aleppo. Naufal gave us all this intelligence, and told us that the Bedouins made constant use of cloaks like ours, black machlas, and above all of cafiés. M. Lascaris accordingly made me buy twenty cloaks, ten machlas, and fifty cafiés, of which I made a bale. This purchase amounted to twelve hundred piastres. Naufal having proposed to us to visit the citadel, the recollection of the adventure at Hama made us at first hesitate; but, on his assurance that nothing disagreeable could happen, and that he would be responsible, we consented, and went with him to view the ruins seated at the top of a small hill in the middle of the town. The castle is in better preservation than that of Hama. We observed in it a deep and concealed grotto, in which was an abundant spring; the water escaped by an opening four feet by two, and passed through bars of iron into a second opening. It is excellent. An old tradition was told us, that the passage being once stopped up, there came a deputation from Persia, which, for a considerable sum paid to the government, procured it to be re-opened, and that for the future the water should not be obstructed. The entrance into the grotto is now forbidden, and it is very difficult to get in.

Returning home, M. Lascaris asked me, if I had noted down what we had seen, and what had occurred since our departure; and on my answer in the negative, he begged that I would do so, making me promise to keep an exact journal in Arabic of all that had occurred, that he might himself translate it into French. From that time I took notes, which he carefully transcribed every day and returned to me the day following. I have now put them together in the hope that they may one day prove useful, and obtain for me a slight compensation for my fatigues and sufferings.

M. Lascaris having determined to go to the village of Saddad, I engaged Naufal to accompany us; and joining some other persons, we quitted Homs with all our merchandise. After five hours' march, we passed a large brook running from north to south towards the castle of Hasné. This castle, commanded by an aga, is a halting-place to the caravan from Mecca to Damascus: the water is excellent for drinking, and we filled our skins with it. This was a necessary precaution, for we found no more on our seven hours' march from thence to Saddad.

We arrived there at sunset. Naufal took us to the sheik, Hassaf Abu Ibrahim, a venerable old man, and father of nine children, all married, and living under the same roof. He received us most kindly, and presented us to all his family, which, to our great astonishment, amounted to sixty-four persons. The sheik having asked us if we wished to establish ourselves in the village, or travel into other countries, we told him we were merchants; that war between the powers having interrupted the communication by sea with Cyprus, we had been desirous of settling at Aleppo, but finding in that city richer merchants than ourselves, we had determined to carry our goods to less frequented places, hoping to make larger gains. Having then told him in what our merchandise consisted, "These articles," said he, "are only useful to the Arabs of the desert; I am sorry to tell you so, but it will be impossible to get to them; and even if you should, you run the risk of losing everything, even your lives. The Bedouins are greedy and audacious; they will seize your goods, and, if you offer the least resistance, will put you to death. You are people of honour and delicacy; you could never put up with their grossness; it is for your sake that I speak thus, being myself a Christian. Take my advice: expose your goods here, sell all that you can, and then return to Aleppo, if you would preserve your property and your lives." He had hardly left off speaking, when the principal people of the village, who had assembled to see us, began telling us alarming stories. One of them said, that a pedler coming from Aleppo, and going into the desert, had been plundered by the Bedouins, and had been seen returning quite naked. Another had learned that a merchant from Damascus had been killed. All agreed as to the impossibility of penetrating amongst the hordes of Bedouins, and endeavoured by every possible means to deter us from the dangerous enterprise.

I saw that M. Lascaris was vexed; he turned to me, and said in Italian, not to be understood by the others, "What say you to this account, which has much discouraged me?" "I do not believe," said I, "all these stories; and even if they were true, we ought still to persevere in our project. Ever since you announced to me your intention to go among the Bedouins, I have never hoped to revisit my home. I regarded the thirty days you allowed me at Aleppo to enjoy myself, as my last farewell of the world; I consider our journey as a real campaign; and he who goes to war, being well resolved, should never think of his return. Let us not lose our courage: though Hassaf is a sheik, and has experience, and understands the cultivation of land and the affairs of his village, he can have no idea of the importance of our business: I therefore am of opinion that we should speak to him no more of our journey into the desert, but place our trust in God, the protector of the universe." These words produced the effect upon M. Lascaris, who embraced me tenderly, and said, "My dear son, I put all my hope in God and in you; you are a man of resolution, I see; I am most satisfied with the strength of your character, and I hope to attain my object by the aid of your courage and constancy." After this conversation, we went to sleep, equally satisfied with one another.

We passed the next day in walking about the village, which contains about two hundred houses and five churches. The inhabitants, Syrian Christians, fabricate machlas and black abas, and pay little attention to agriculture, from want of water, which is sensibly felt. There is only one little spring in the village, the distribution of the water being regulated by an hour-glass. It scarcely suffices to water the gardens, which, in a climate where it seldom rains, are unproductive without watering. Some years there does not fall a drop of rain. The produce of the soil is hardly enough for six months' consumption; and, for the remainder of the year, the inhabitants are obliged to have recourse to Homs. In the middle of the village there arises an ancient tower of prodigious height. It dates from the foundation of a colony whose history the sheik told us. The founders were natives of Tripoli in Syria, where their church still exists. At the most flourishing period of the Eastern empire, the Greeks, full of pride and rapacity, tyrannised over the conquered people. The governor of Tripoli overwhelmed the inhabitants with exactions and cruelty; these, too few to resist, and unable to bear the yoke, concerted together to the number of three hundred families; and having secretly collected together all the valuables they could carry away, they departed without noise in the middle of the night, went to Homs, and from thence moved towards the desert of Bagdad, where they were overtaken by the Greek troops sent in pursuit of them by the governor of Tripoli. They made an obstinate and sanguinary resistance; but too inferior in numbers to conquer, and resolved on no account to submit any longer to the tyranny of the Greeks, they entered into negotiation, and obtained permission to build a village on the spot of the battle, agreeing to remain tributary to the governor of Tripoli. They established themselves at this place, at the entrance of the desert, and called their village Saddad (obstacle.) This is all that the Syrian chronicle contains worthy of remark.

The inhabitants of Saddad are brave, but gentle. We unpacked our goods, and spent some days with them, to prove that we were really merchants. The women bought much of our red cotton cloth, to make chemises. The sale did not detain us long, but we were obliged to await the arrival of the Bedouins in the environs. One day, having been told that there was four hours from the village a considerable ruin, and very ancient, in which was a natural vapour bath, the wonder excited our curiosity; and M. Lascaris, desirous of seeing it, begged the sheik to give us an escort. After marching four hours to the southeast, we arrived in the midst of an extensive ruin, in which there remains only one habitable room. The architecture is simple; but the stones are of prodigious size. On entering the room, we perceived an opening two feet square, from which issued a thick vapour; we threw into it a handkerchief, and in a minute and a half, by the watch, it was thrown out and fell at our feet. We repeated the experiment with a shirt, which, at the end of ten minutes, returned like the handkerchief. Our guides assured us that a machlas, which weighs ten pounds, would be thrown up in the same manner.

Having undressed, and placed ourselves around the opening, we were in a short time covered with perspiration, which trickled down our bodies; but the smell of the vapour was so detestable, that we could not remain a long time exposed to it. After half an hour we put on our clothes, and experienced a most delightful sensation. We were told that the vapour was really very sanative, and cured numbers of sick. Returning to the village, we supped with an excellent appetite; and never, perhaps, did I enjoy a more delicious sleep.

Having nothing more to see at Saddad, or the neighbourhood, we determined to set out for the village of Corietain. When we spoke of this to Naufal, he advised us to change our names, as our own would create suspicion in the Bedouins and the Turks. From that time M. Lascaris took the name of Sheik Ibrahim el Cabressi (the Cyprian,) and gave me that of Abdallah el Katib.

Sheik Hassaf having given us a letter of recommendation to a Syrian curate named Moussi, we took leave of him and our friends at Saddad, and set off early. After four hours, we came between the two villages of Mahim and Haourin, ten minutes apart: each contains about twenty houses, mostly ruined by the Bedouins, who come from time to time to plunder them. In the midst of these villages is a lofty tower of ancient construction. The inhabitants, all Mussulmans, speak the language of the Bedouins, and dress like them. After having breakfasted and filled our water-bottles, we continued our journey for six hours, and about nightfall arrived at Corietain, at the curate Moussi's, who afforded us hospitality. The next day he conducted us to the Sheik Selim el Dahasse, a distinguished person, who received us very kindly. Having learned the motive of our journey, he made the same observation as the Sheik of Saddad. We answered him, "that, aware of the difficulties of the enterprise, we had given up the idea of penetrating into the desert, and should be satisfied with going to Palmyra, to dispose of our merchandise."—"That will be still too difficult," added he, "for the Bedouins may still meet you and pillage you." He then began, in his turn, to repeat a thousand alarming things about the Bedouins. The curate confirming all he said, contributed to damp our spirits; when breakfast was served, which changed the conversation, and gave us time to recover.

Sheik Selim is one of those who are bound to supply the wants of the great caravan to Mecca, in conjunction with the Sheik of Palmyra: and his office gives him some influence over the Arabs: his contingent consists of two hundred camels and provisions. On our return home, Sheik Ibrahim, addressing me, said, "Well, my son, what do you think of all we have heard from Sheik Selim?"—"We must not," said I, "pay too much regard to all that the inhabitants of these villages tell us, who are always at war with the Bedouins; there cannot exist much harmony between them. Our position is very different; we are merchants,—we go to sell them our goods, and not to make war: by acting honourably towards them, I do not apprehend the least danger." These words reassured Sheik Ibrahim.

Some days after our arrival, in order to support our character of merchants, we opened our bales in the middle of the village, before the doors of the sheik: I sold to the women some articles, which were paid for in money. The idle people were standing around us to talk; one of them, very young, named Hessaisoun el Katib, helped me to take the money, and settle the accounts with the women and children: he showed great zeal for my interests. One day, finding me alone, he asked me if I was able to keep a secret. "Be careful," said he; "it is a great secret that you must trust to nobody, not even to your companion." Having given him my word, he told me that one hour from the village was a grotto, in which was a large jar filled with sequins; he gave me one, assuring me that he could not employ the money, which was not current at Palmyra. "But you," continued he, "are going from city to city, and can change it easily; you have a thousand ways of profiting by the treasure that I have not: however, I will not give you the whole, but I shall leave the division to your generosity: you shall come with me to reconnoitre the spot; we can remove the gold by degrees and in secret, and you shall give me my share in the current coin." Having seen and handled the sequin, I believed in the truth of the story, and gave him a meeting early the following morning outside the village.

The next morning by daylight I arose, and went from the house as if to walk. At some paces from the village I found Hessaisoun, who was waiting for me: he was armed with a gun, a sabre, and pistols; I had no other arms than a long pipe. We proceeded onwards for an hour. With what impatience did I look out for the grotto!—at last I perceived it. We soon entered: I looked on all sides to discover the jar; and not seeing any, I turned towards Hessaisoun— "Where is the jar?" said I,—I saw him grow pale—"Since we are here," exclaimed he, "learn that thy last hour is come. Thou shouldst have been dead already, were I not afraid of soiling thy clothes with blood. Before I kill thee, I will despoil thee; so give me thy bag of money: I know thou hast it about thee: it must contain more than twelve hundred piastres, which I counted myself, the price of the goods sold. Thou shalt see no more the light of day."

"Give me my life," said I, in a supplicating tone, "and I will give thee a much larger sum than that in the sack, and will tell no one of what has passed—I swear to thee."—"That cannot be," said he; "this grotto shall be thy grave. I cannot give thee thy life without exposing my own."

I swore to him a thousand times that I would be silent: I offered to give him a bill for whatever sum he should fix;—nothing could move him from his fearful project. At length, tired by my resistance, he placed his arms against the wall and darted upon me like an enraged lion, to undress me before killing me. I entreated him again—"What harm have I done you?" said I,—"what enmity is there between us? You do not know, then, that the day of judgment is at hand—that God will demand the blood of the innocent?"—But his hardened heart listened to nothing. I thought of my brother, my parents, my friends; all that was dear to me came to my mind;—desperate, I no longer prayed for protection but from my Creator. "O God! protector of the innocent! help me! give me strength to resist!" My assassin, impatient, snatched my clothes: although he was much bigger than I, God gave me strength to struggle with him for more than half an hour: the blood flowed abundantly from my face—my clothes were torn to rags. The villain, seeing me in this state, endeavoured to strangle me, and raised his arm to grasp my neck. I took advantage of the liberty this movement allowed me, to give him with both fists a violent blow in the stomach: I knocked him backwards, and seizing his arms, I darted out of the grotto, running with all my might. I could scarcely believe the happiness of being saved. Some moments afterwards I heard a running after me: it was the assassin. He called to me, begging me to wait in the most conciliating tone. Having all his arms, I no longer feared to stop, and turning towards him, "Wretch," said I, "what is it you ask?—you would have assassinated me in secret; but it is you who will be strangled in public." He answered me by affirming with an oath, that it had all been a jest on his part; that he had wanted to try my courage, and see how I would defend myself. "But I see," added he, "that you are but a child, since you take it so."—I answered, raising the gun, that if he came a step nearer I would shoot him. Seeing that I was determined to do it, he fled across the desert, and I returned to the village.

In the meantime, Sheik Ibrahim, the curate, and Naufal, not finding me return, began to be alarmed. Sheik Ibrahim above all, knowing that I never went to a distance without acquainting him, after two hours' delay went to the sheik, who, participating in his anxiety, sent out all the village in search of me. At last Naufal, perceiving me, cried out: "There he is!" Selim thought he was mistaken. I drew nearer: they could with difficulty recognise me. M. Lascaris embraced me and wept: I was unable to speak. They took me to the curate's, bathed my wounds and put me to bed. At length I found strength to relate my adventure. Selim sent horsemen in pursuit of the assassin, giving to the negro the rope that was to strangle him; but they returned without being able to overtake him, and we soon learned that he had entered the service of the

Pacha of Damascus. He never returned to Corietain.

At the end of a few days my wounds began to heal, and I soon recovered my strength. Sheik Selim, who had conceived a great friendship for me, brought me a telescope that was out of order, telling me I should be a clever fellow if I could mend it. As there was only a glass to replace, I restored it and brought it to him. He was so pleased with my skill, that he gave me the surname of "the industrious."

In a short time we learnt that the Bedouins were approaching Palmyra: some were seen even in the environs of Corietain. Presently there came one, named Selame el Hassan. We were at Selim's when he entered: coffee was brought, and while we were taking it, many of the inhabitants came to the sheik, and said: "Eight years ago, at such a place, Hassan killed our relative; and we are come to demand justice." Hassan denied the fact, and asked if they had witnesses. "No," they replied; "but you were seen passing alone on the road, and a little after we found our relative lying dead. We know that there existed a cause of hatred between you: it is therefore clear that you are his assassin." Hassan still denied the charge: and the sheik, who from fear was obliged to exercise caution with the Bedouins, and besides had no positive proof in the case, took a piece of wood and said, "By Him who created this stem, swear that you have not killed their relation." Hassan took the wood, looked at it some minutes, and bent down his head; then raising it towards his accusers, "I will not have," said he, "two crimes on my heart,—the one of being the murderer of this man, the other of swearing falsely before God. It is I who have killed your kinsman: what do you demand for the price of his blood?"* The sheik, from policy, would not act according to the full rigour of the law; and the persons present being interested in the negotiation, it was decided that Hassan should pay three hundred piastres to the relations of the dead. When it came to the payment of the money, he said he had it not about him, but that he would bring it in a few days; and as some difficulty was made of letting him go without security, "I have no pledge," said he, "to give; but He will answer for me whose name I would not profane by a false oath." He departed; and four days afterwards returned with fifteen sheep, each worth above twenty piastres.—This trait of good faith and generosity at once charmed and surprised us. We wished to make acquaintance with Hassan: Sheik Ibrahim invited him, gave him a few presents, and we became intimate friends. He told us that he belonged to the tribe El-Ammour, whose chief was Sultan el Brrak. This tribe, composed of five hundred tents, is considered as constituting part of the country, because it never quits the banks of the Euphrates when the great tribes retire. They sell sheep, camels, and butter, at Damascus, Homs, Hama, &c. The inhabitants

* According to Arab law, murder is compensated by money; and the sum is fixed according to circumstances.

of these different cities have often a concern in their flocks.

We one day said to Hassan that we were desirous of going to Palmyra to sell our remaining merchandise, but that we had been alarmed by the dangers of the road. Having offered to conduct us, he made a note before the sheik, by which he made himself responsible for all the disasters that might happen. Being satisfied that Hassan was a man of honour, we accepted his proposal.

Spring was come, and the desert, lately so arid, was all at once covered with a carpeting of verdure and flowers. This enchanting spectacle induced us to hasten our departure. The night before, we deposited at the curate Moussi's a part of our goods, in order not to awaken either curiosity or cupidity. Naufal wished to return to Homs, and M. Lascaris dismissed him with a liberal recompense; and the next day, having hired some moukres, with their camels, we took leave of the people of Corietain, and having provided water and provisions for two days, we departed betimes, carrying a letter of recommendation from Sheik Selim to the Sheik of Palmyra, whose name was Ragial el Orouk.

After a ten hours' march, always towards the east, we stopped at a square tower, extremely lofty and of massive construction, called Casser el Ourdaan, on the territory El Dawh. This tower, built in the time of the Greek empire, served for an advanced post against the Persians, who came to carry off the inhabitants of the country. This bulwark of the desert has preserved its name till these times. After having admired its architecture, which belongs to a good period, we returned to pass the night at our little khan, where we suffered much from the cold. In the morning, as we were preparing to depart, M. Lascaris, not yet accustomed to the movements of camels, mounted his without care; which rising suddenly, threw him down. We ran to him: his leg appeared to be dislocated; but, as he would not be detained, after having done what we could, we replaced him on his seat, and continued our route. We proceeded for two hours, when we observed at a distance a cloud of dust approaching us, and soon were able to distinguish six armed horsemen. Hardly had Hassan perceived them, when he threw off his cloak, took his lance and ran to meet them, crying out to us not to go forward. Having come up to them, he told them that we were merchants going to Palmyra, and that he had engaged before Sheik Selim and all his village to conduct us thither in safety. But these Bedouins, of the tribe El Hassnnee, without listening to him, came up to us: Hassan threw himself forward to stop the road; they attempted to drive him back, and a battle began. Our defender was known for his valour, but his opponents were equally brave. He sustained the attack for half an hour, and at length, wounded by a lance which pierced his thigh, he retired towards us, and soon fell from his horse. The Bedouins were beginning to plunder us, when Hassan, extended on the ground, the blood flowing from his wound, apostrophised them in these terms:—

"What are you about, my friends?—will you then violate the laws of Arabs, the usages of the Bedouins? They whom you are plundering are my brethren—they have my word; I am responsible for all that may befall them, and you are robbing them!—is this according to honour?"

"Why," said they, "did you undertake to convey Christians to Palmyra? Know you not that Mehanna el Fadel (the sheik of their tribe) is chief of the country? Why did you not ask his permission?"

"I know," replied Hassan; "but these merchants were in haste; Mehanna is far from this. I have pledged my word—they believed me; they know our laws and our usages, which never change. Is it worthy of you to violate them, by despoiling these strangers, and leaving me wounded in this manner?"

At these words the Bedouins, ceasing their violence, answered, "All that you say is true and just; and as it is so, we will take from thy protégés only what they choose to give us."

We made all haste to offer them two machlas, a cloak, and a hundred piastres. They were satisfied, and left us to pursue our route. Hassan suffered a great deal from his wound; and as he could not remount his horse, I gave him my camel, and took his mare. We proceeded for four hours; but the sun being set, we were obliged to halt at a place called Waddi el Nahr (Valley of the River.) However, there was not a drop of water in it, and our skins were empty: the attack in the morning had detained us three hours, and it was impossible to go further that night.

Notwithstanding all we had to suffer, we were still very happy at having escaped the Bedouins, and preserved our clothes, which secured us a little from the cold wind, that affected us sensibly. In short, between pleasure and pain, we watched with impatience for the dawn of day. Sheik Ibrahim suffered from his foot, and Hassan from his wound. In the morning, having disposed of our sick in the best manner we could, we again set forward, and still towards the east. At an hour and a quarter from Palmyra we found a subterraneous stream, the spring of which is entirely unknown, as well as the place where it is lost. The water is seen to flow through openings of about five feet, forming a sort of basins. It is unnecessary to say with what delight we quenched our thirst:—the water appeared excellent.

At the entrance of a pass formed by the junction of two mountains, we'at length perceived the celebrated Palmyra. This defile forms for a quarter of an hour an avenue to the city; along the mountain on the south side extends for almost three hours a very ancient rampart. Facing you to the left is an old castle, built by the Turks after the invention of gunpowder. It is called Co Lat Ebn Maâen.—This Ebn Maâen, a governor of Damascus in the time of the Khalifs, had built the castle to prevent the Persians from penetrating into Syria.—We next arrived at a vast space, called Waddi el Cabour (Valley of the Tombs.) The sepulchres that cover it appear at a distance like towers. On coming near, we saw that niches had been cut in them to enclose the dead. Every niche is shut up by a stone, on which is carved a portrait of its occupant. The towers have three or four stories, communicating by means of a staircase, commonly in good preservation. From thence we came into a vast enclosure inhabited by the Arabs, who call it the Castle. It contains, in fact, the ruins of the Temple of the Sun. Two hundred families reside in these ruins. We immediately presented ourselves to Sheik Ragial el Orouk, a venerable old man, who received us well, and made us sup and sleep with him. This sheik, like the sheik of Corietain, furnishes two hundred camels to the great caravan of Mecca.

The following day, having hired a house, we unpacked our goods. I attended to the foot of Sheik Ibrahim, which was in reality dislocated. He had long to suffer the pain. Hassan found friends at Palmyra who took care of him; and being soon recovered, he came to take leave of us, and went away delighted with the manner in which we recompensed him.

Being obliged to keep at home for several days on account of Sheik Ibrahim's foot, we set about selling some articles, to confirm our mercantile character. But as soon as M. Lascaris was in a fit state to walk, we went to visit the temple in all its minutiæ. Other travellers have described the ruins: therefore we will only speak of what may have escaped their observation relating to the country.

We one day saw many people engaged in surrounding with wood a beautiful granite column. We were told it was to burn it, or rather to cause it to fall, in order to obtain the lead which was in the joinings. Sheik Ibrahim, full of indignation, addressing me, exclaimed, "What would the founders of Palmyra say if they beheld these barbarians thus destroying their work? Since chance has brought me hither, I will oppose this act of Vandalism." And having learned what might be the worth of the lead, he gave the fifty piastres they asked, and the column became our property. It was of the most beautiful red granite, spotted with blue and black, sixty-two feet in length, and ten in circumference. The Palmyrians, perceiving our taste for monuments, pointed out to us a curious spot, an hour and a half distant, in which the columns were formerly cut, and where there are still some beautiful fragments. For ten piastres three Arabs agreed to take us there. The road is strewed with very beautiful ruins, described, I presume, by other travellers. We observed a grotto, in which was a beautiful white marble column cut and chiselled, and another only half finished. One might say that Time, the destroyer of so much magnificence, was wanting to place up the first, and to finish the second.

After having been into several grottoes, and visited the neighbourhood, we came back by another road. Our guides pointed out a beautiful spring, covered with blocks of stone. It is called Ain Ournus. The name struck Sheik Ibrahim. At last, calling me, he said: "I have discovered what this name Ournus means. Aurelianus, the Roman emperor, came to besiege Palmyra and take possession of its riches. It is he probably who dug this well for the wants of his army during the siege, and the spring may have taken his name, changed by the lapse of time into Ournus." According to my feeble knowledge of history, Sheik Ibrahim's conjecture is not without foundation.

The inhabitants of Palmyra are but little occupied about agriculture. Their chief employment is the working of a salt-mine, the produce of which they send to Damascus and Homs. They also make a great deal of Soda. The plant that furnishes it is very abundant: it is burnt, and the ashes are also sent to those towns to make soap. They are even sent sometimes as far as Tripoli in Syria, where there are many soap manufactories, and which supply the Archipelago.

We were one day informed of a very curious grotto; but the entrance to it, being dark and narrow, was hardly practicable. It was three hours from Palmyra. We felt a wish to see it; but my adventure with Hessaisoun was too recent to commit ourselves without a strong escort: therefore we begged Sheik Ragial to furnish us with trusty people. Astonished at our project, "You are very curious," said he: "what does the grotto signify to you? Instead of attending to your business, you pass your time in this trifling. Never did I see such merchants as you."—"Man always profits," said I, "by seeing all the beauties that nature has created." The sheik having given us six men well armed,

I provided myself with a ball of thread, a large nail, and torches, and we set out very early in the morning. After two hours' march we reached the foot of a mountain. A great hole that they showed us formed the entrance of the grotto. I stuck my nail into a place out of sight, and holding the ball in my hand, followed Sheik Ibrahim and the guides who carried the torches. We went on, sometimes to the right, sometimes to the left, then up and then down; in short, the grotto is large enough to accommodate an entire army. We found a good deal of alum. The vault and the sides of the rock were covered with sulphur, and the bottom with nitre. We remarked a species of red earth, very fine, of an acid taste. Sheik Ibrahim put a handful into his handkerchief. The grotto is full of cavities cut out with a chisel, whence metals were anciently taken. Our guides told us of many persons who had lost themselves in it and perished. A man had remained there two days in vain looking for the outlet, when he saw a wolf: he threw stones at him; and having put him to flight, followed him, and so found the opening. My length of cord being exhausted, we would not go further, but retraced our steps. The charm of curiosity had, without doubt, smoothed the way, for we had infinite difficulty in gaining the outlet.

As soon as we were out, we hastened our breakfast, and took the road to Palmyra. The sheik, who was expecting us, asked us what we had gained by the journey. "We have learned," said I, "that the ancients were more skilful than we; for it may be seen by their works that they could go in and out with ease, whilst we had great difficulty in extricating ourselves."

He set up a laugh, and we quitted him to go and rest ourselves. At night Sheik Ibrahim found the handkerchief, in which he had put the red earth, all in holes and rotten. The earth had fallen into his pocket. He put it into a bottle,* and told me that probably the ancients had obtained gold from this grotto. Chemical experience proves that where there is sulphur there is often gold ; and besides, the great works we had remarked could not have been made merely to extract sulphur and alum, but evidently something more precious. If the Arabs had suspected that we were going to search for gold, our lives would not have been safe.

From day to day we heard of the approach of the Bedouins, and Sheik Ibrahim was as rejoiced as if he was about to see his countrymen. He was enchanted when I announced to him the arrival of the great Bedouin prince, Mehanna el Fadel. He wished immediately to go to meet him: but I represented to him, that it would be more prudent to wait a favourable opportunity of seeing some one of the emir's (prince's) family. I knew that, ordinarily, Mehanna sent a messenger to the Sheik of Palmyra to announce to him his approach. In fact, I witnessed the arrival one day of eleven Bedouin horsemen, and learned that the Emir Nasser was amongst them, the eldest son of Mehanna. I ran to carry the intelligence to Sheik Ibrahim, who seemed at the

* This bottle was taken with all the rest into Egypt.

height of joy. Immediately we went to Sheik Ragial, to present us to the Emir Nasser, who gave us a kind reception. "These strangers," said Ragial to him, "are honest merchants, who have goods to sell useful to the Bedouins; but they have so frightened them, that they dare not venture into the desert unless you will grant them your protection."

The emir, turning towards us, said :—"Hope for all sorts of prosperity: you shall be welcome; and I promise you that nothing shall befall you but the rain which descends from heaven." We offered him many thanks, saying, "Since we have had the advantage of making your acquaintance, and you will be our protector, you will do us the honour of eating with us?"

The Arabs in general, and above all the Bedouins, regard it as an inviolable pledge of fidelity to have eaten with any one—even to have broken bread with him. We therefore invited him, with all his suite, as well as the sheik. We killed a sheep, and the dinner, dressed in the manner of the Bedouins, appeared to them excellent. At dessert we offered them figs, raisins, almonds, and nuts, which was a great treat to them. After coffee, when we began to speak of different things, we related to Nasser our adventure with the six horsemen of his tribe. He wished to punish them and restore our money. We earnestly conjured him not to do so, assuring him we attached no value to what we had given. We would have departed with him the next day, but he induced us to await the arrival of his father, who was at eight days' distance. He promised to send us an escort, and camels to carry our merchandise. For a greater security, we begged him to write by his father, which he engaged to do.

The second day after, there arrived at Palmyra a Bedouin of the tribe El Hassnnee, named Bani; and some hours after, seven others of the tribe El Daffir, with which that of Hassnnee is at war. These having learned that there was one of their enemies in the city, resolved to wait for him out of the town to kill him. Bani having been told this, came to us, tied his mare to our door, and begged us to lend him a felt. We had several which wrapped our merchandise; I brought him one. He put it to soak in water for half an hour, and then placed it, wet as it was, on his mare's back, underneath the saddle. Two hours afterwards she had a strong diarrhœa, which lasted all the evening, and the next day seemed to have nothing in her body. Bani then took off the felt, which he returned, well girthed his seat, and departed.

About four hours after noon we saw the Bedouins of the tribe El Daffir return without booty. Some one having asked them what they had done with the mare of Bani, "This," said they, "is what has happened to us. Not wishing to commit an insult towards Ragial, a tributary of Mehanna, we abstained from attacking our enemy in the city. We might have waited for him in a narrow pass; but we were seven to one: we therefore resolved to wait for him in the open plain. Having perceived him, we ran upon him; but as soon as he was in the midst of us, he uttered a loud cry, saying to his horse, '*Jah Hamra!*—It is now thy turn,'—and he flew off like lightning. We followed him to his tribe without being able to catch him, astonished at the swiftness of his mare, which seemed like a bird cleaving the air with its wings." I then told them the history of the felt, which caused them much wonder, having, said they, no idea of such sorcery.

Eight days after, three men came to us from Mehanna el Fadel: they came to us with the camels, and put into our hands a letter from himself; these are the contents:—

"Mehanna el Fadel, the son of Melkhgem, to Sheik Ibrahim and Abdalla el Katib, greeting. May the mercy of God be upon you! On the arrival of our son Nasser, we were informed of the desire you have to visit us. Be welcome! you will shed blessing upon us. Fear nothing; you have the protection of God, and the word of Mehanna; nothing shall touch you but the rain of heaven! Signed, MEHANNA EL FFADEL."

A seal was appended by the side of the signature. The letter gave great pleasure to Sheik Ibrahim: our preparations were soon made, and early the next morning we were out of Palmyra. Being arrived at a village watered by an abundant spring, we filled our skins for the rest of the route. This village, called Arak, is four hours from Palmyra. We met a great number of Bedouins, who, after having questioned our conductors, continued their road. After a march of ten hours, the plain appeared covered with fifteen hundred tents: it was the tribe of Mehanna. We entered into the tent of the emir, who ordered us coffee at three different intervals; which, amongst the Bedouins, is the greatest proof of consideration. After the third cup, supper was served, which we were obliged to eat *a la Turque:* it was the first time this had occurred, so that we burnt our fingers. Mehanna perceived it.

"You are not accustomed," said he, "to eat as we do."—"It is true," replied Sheik Ibrahim; "but why do you not make use of spoons? it is always possible to procure them, if only of wood."—"We are Bedouins," replied the emir, "and we keep to the customs of our ancestors, which, besides, we consider well founded. The hand and the mouth are the parts of the body that God has given us to aid each other. Why then make use of a strange thing, whether of wood or of metal, to reach the mouth, when the hand is naturally made for that purpose?" We were obliged to approve these reasons, and I remarked to Sheik Ibrahim that Mehanna was the first Bedouin philosopher that we had encountered.

The next day the emir had a camel killed to regale us, and I learned that that was a high mark of consideration, the Bedouins measuring the importance of the stranger by the animal they kill to welcome him. They begin with a lamb, and finish with a camel. This was the first time we had eaten the flesh of this animal, and we thought it rather insipid.

The Emir Mehanna was a man of eighty years

of age, little, thin, deaf, and very ill-clothed. His great influence among the Bedouins arises from his noble and generous heart, and from being the chief of a very ancient and numerous family. He is entrusted by the Pacha of Damascus with the escort of the grand caravan to Mecca, for twenty-five purses (twelve thousand five hundred piastres,) which are paid him before their departure from Damascus. He has three sons, Nasser, Faress, and Hamed, all married, and inhabiting the same tent as their father. This tent is seventy-two feet long, and as many wide; it is of black horsehair, and divided into three partitions. In the further one is kept the provisions, and there the cookery is performed; the slaves, too, sleep there. The middle is kept for the women, and all the family retire to it at night. The fore part is occupied by the men: in this strangers are received: this part is called Rabha.

After three days devoted to enjoying their hospitality, we opened our bales, and sold many articles, upon most of which we lost more or less. I did not understand this mode of dealing, and said so to Sheik Ibrahim. "Have you then forgot our conditions?" said he. I excused myself, and continued to sell according to his pleasure.

One day we saw arrive fifty well-mounted horsemen, who, having stopped before the tents, dismounted and sat on the ground. The Emir Nasser, charged with all the affairs since his father had become deaf, went to join them, accompanied by his cousin Sheik Zamel, and held a conference with them for two hours, after which the men remounted their horses and departed. Sheik Ibrahim, anxious about this mysterious interview, knew not how to ascertain the motive of it. Having already been often with the women, I took a coral necklace, and went to Naura, the wife of Nasser, to present it to her. She accepted it, made me sit near her, and offered me in her turn dates and coffee. After these reciprocal acts of politeness, I came to the object of my visit, and said, "Excuse my importunity, I entreat you, but strangers are curious and timid; the little merchandise we have here is the remnant of a considerable fortune, which misfortunes have deprived us of. The Emir Nasser was just now holding conference with strangers—that excites our apprehension; we would know the subject."—"I will satisfy your curiosity," said Naura; "but on condition that you will keep my secret, and appear to know nothing. Know that my husband has many enemies among the Bedouins, who hate him for humbling the national pride by exalting the power of the Turks. The alliance of Nasser with the Osmanlis greatly displeases the Bedouins, who hate them. It is even contrary to the advice of his father, and the heads of the tribe, who murmur against him. The object of this meeting was to concert a plan of attack. To-morrow they will assail the tribe El Daffir, to take their flocks, and do them all the mischief possible: the God of battle will give the victory to whom he pleases: but as to you, you have nothing to fear." Having thanked Naura, I withdrew well satisfied with having gained her confidence.

Sheik Ibrahim, informed by me of all the wife of Nasser had told me, said that it caused him the greatest vexation. "I was endeavouring," added he, "to attach myself to a tribe hostile to the Osmanlis, and here I am with a chief allied to them." I did not dare ask the meaning of these words, but they served to set me thinking.

About sunset three hundred horsemen assembled beyond the encampment, and marched early in the morning, having at their head Nasser, Hamed, and Zamel. Three days afterwards a messenger came to announce their return. A great number of men and women went out to meet them; and when they had reached them, they sent up on both sides loud shouts of joy, and in this manner made their triumphal entry into the camp, preceded by a hundred and eighty camels, taken from the enemy. As soon as they had alighted, we begged them to recount their exploit.

"The day after our departure," said Nasser, "having arrived about noon at the place where the shepherds feed the flocks of Daffir, we fell upon them, and carried off a hundred and eighty camels: however, the shepherds having fled, gave the alarm to their tribe. I then detached a part of my troops to conduct our booty to the camp by another road. Aruad-Ebn-Motlac, the chief of the tribe El Daffir, coming to attack us with three hundred horsemen, the battle lasted two hours, and night alone separated us. Every one then returned to his tribe, the enemy having lost one of his men, and we having two men wounded."

The tribe of Nasser feigned a participation in his triumph, whereas in reality they were very dissatisfied with an unjust war against their natural friends, to please the Osmanlis. Nasser, having visited all the chiefs, to recount his success, came to Sheik Ibrahim and addressed him in Turkish; Sheik Ibrahim having observed to him that he spoke only Greek, his native tongue, and a little Arabic, Nasser began to extol the language and customs of the Turks, saying it was not possible to be truly great, powerful, and respected, without being on a good footing with them. "As for me," added he, "I am more Osmanli than Bedouin." "Trust not the promises of the Turks," replied Sheik Ibrahim, "any more than their greatness and magnificence: they favour you that they may gain you over, and injure you with your countrymen, in order to employ you to fight against the other tribes. The interest of the Turkish government is to destroy the Bedouins: not strong enough to effect this themselves, they wish to arm you against each other. Take care that you have not some day cause to repent. I give you this advice as a friend who takes a lively interest in you, and because I have eaten your bread and partaken of your hospitality."

Some time after, Nasser received from Soliman, the pacha of Acre and Damascus, a message, engaging him to come and receive the investiture of the general command of all the desert, with the title of Prince of the Bedouins.

This message overwhelmed him with joy, and he departed for Damascus with ten horsemen.

Mehanna having ordered the departure of the tribe, the next morning by sunrise not a single tent was to be seen standing; all was folded up and loaded, and the departure began in the greatest order. Twenty chosen horsemen formed the advanced guard, and served as scouts. Then came the camels with their loads, and the flocks; then the armed men, mounted on horses or camels; after these the women; those of the chiefs carried in howdahs, (a sort of palankin,) placed on the backs of the largest camels. These howdahs are very rich, carefully lined, covered with scarlet cloth, and ornamented with different coloured fringe. They hold commodiously two women, or a woman and several children. The women and children of inferior rank follow directly after, seated on rolls of tent-cloth, ranged like seats, and placed on camels. The loaded camels, carrying the baggage and provision, are behind. The line was closed by the Emir Mehanna, mounted on a dromedary by reason of his great age, and surrounded by his slaves, the rest of the warriors, and the servants, who were on foot. It was truly wonderful to witness the order and celerity with which the departure of eight or nine thousand persons was effected. Sheik Ibrahim and I were on horseback, sometimes ahead, sometimes in the centre, or by the side of Mehanna. We proceeded ten hours successively: all at once, three hours after noon, the order of march was interrupted; the Bedouins dispersed themselves in the midst of a fine plain, sprang to the ground, fixed their lances, and fastened their horses to them. The women ran on all sides, and pitched their tents near their husbands' horses. Thus, as if by enchantment, we found ourselves in a kind of city, as large as Hama. It is the duty of the women alone to pitch and to strike the tents, and they acquit themselves with surprising address and rapidity. All the labours of the encampment generally fall to the lot of the women. The men take charge of the flocks, kill and skin the beasts. The costume of the women is very simple; they wear a large blue chemise, a black machlas, and a sort of black silk scarf, which, after covering the head, passes twice round the neck, and falls over the back. They have no covering for the legs; except the wives of the sheiks, who wear yellow boots. Their great ambition and luxury is to have a great many bracelets; they have them of glass, of coral, coin, and amber.

The plain on which we rested was called El Makram. It is not far from Hama. The place is rather agreeable, and its rich pasturage renders it suitable to the Bedouins.

The fourth day we had an alarm: four hours after noon the shepherds came running in haste, crying "To arms! the enemy are seizing our flocks." It was the tribe of Daflir, who, watching the opportunity to revenge themselves on Nasser, had sent a thousand horse to carry off the flocks at nightfall, to allow no time for a pursuit. Our men, expecting an attack, were prepared; but it was necessary to find out on which side the enemy were. Night coming on, four men dismounted from their horses, took opposite directions, and crouching down, their ears close to the ground, heard at a great distance the steps of the plunderers. Night passed without being able to reach them; but in the morning the troop of Hassné (that of Mehanna) having joined them, they gave battle. After four hours' fighting, half the flocks were recaptured: but five hundred camels remained in the hands of the tribe El Daffir. We had ten men killed and several wounded. At the return, the affliction was general; the Bedouins murmured, attributing all that had happened to the caprice and vanity of Nasser.

Mehanna sent off a courier to his son, who immediately returned from Damascus, accompanied by a chokedar, (an officer of the pacha,) in order to make an impression on the Bedouins. On his arrival he read a letter from the pacha, to the following effect:—

"We make known to all the emirs and sheiks of the desert, great and small, encamped on the territory of Damascus, that we have appointed our son, Nasser Ebn Mehanna, Emir of all the Anazes (Bedouins of the desert,) inviting them to obey him. The tribe that shall have the misfortune to show itself rebellious, shall be destroyed by our victorious troops, and, as an example, their flocks shall be slaughtered, and their women delivered up to the soldiers. Such is our will.   Signed,
"SOLIMAN, Pacha of Damascus and Acre."

Nasser, proud of his new dignity, affected to read the order to every body, and to talk Turkish with the officer of the pacha, which still further increased the disgust of the Bedouins. One day whilst we were with him, there arrived a very handsome young man, named Zarrak, the chief of a neighbouring tribe. Nasser, as usual, spoke of his appointment, vaunted the greatness and power of the vizier of Damascus, and of the sultan of Constantinople " of the long sabre."*
Zarrak, who listened with impatience, changing colour, rose and said, "Nasser Aga,† learn that all the Bedouins detest thee: if thou art dazzled by the magnificence of the Turks, go to Damascus; adorn thy forehead with the caouk;‡ become the minister of the vizier; dwell in his palace; perhaps thou mayest strike terror into the Damascenes; but we Bedouins care no more for thee, thy vizier and thy sultan, than camel dung. I shall depart for the territory of Bagdad, where I shall find the Drayhy§ Ebn Chahllan; him will I join."

Nasser, in his turn growing pale with anger, transmitted the conversation in Turkish to the chokedar, who thought by violent menaces to alarm Zarrak. But he, looking at him fiercely, said, "It is enough: though you have Nasser on your side, I could, if I would, prevent you from ever eating bread more." In spite of

* An Arabic expression implying extent of dominion.
† A title of a Turkish officer, used in derision by the Bedouins.
‡ Turban of ceremony, (Turkish.)
§ Destroyer of the Turks.

these offensive words, all three preserved their coolness; and Zarrak, mounting his horse, said to Nasser, "*Salam aleik* (peace to thee); display all thy power; I await thee." This challenge caused Nasser much trouble; but he still persevered in his alliance with the Turks.

The following day we learned that Zarrak had set out with his tribe for the country of Geziri, and a combination of the Bedouins against Nasser was talked of in all quarters. Mehanna, having learned what was passing, called his son to him, and said, "Nasser, will you then break the pillars of the tent of Melkhgem?" and taking his beard in his hand, "Will you," added he, "bring contempt upon this beard at the end of my days, and tarnish the reputation I have acquired? Unhappy man, thou hast not invoked the name of God. What I had foreseen, has happened. All the tribes will unite with the Drayhy. What then will become of us? It will only remain for us to humble ourselves before Ebn Sihoud, that enemy of our race, who styles himself king of the Bedouins; he alone can defend us from the terrible Drayhy."

Nasser endeavoured to tranquillize his father, assuring him that matters were not so bad as he feared. However, the Bedouins began to take part with one or the other; but the greater part sided with the father, who was in their true interest.

Sheik Ibrahim was very dissatisfied; he wished to penetrate farther into the desert, and proceed as far as Bagdad; and he found himself bound to a tribe that remained between Damascus and

Homs. He thus lost all the summer, being able to remove only with danger of his life. He desired me to obtain some knowledge respecting the Drayhy, to learn his character, the places where he passed the summer, where he wintered, if he received strangers, and many other particulars; in short, he told me he had the greatest interest in being rightly informed.

These details were difficult to obtain without exciting suspicion: it was necessary to find some one not of the tribe of El Hassnnee. At length I became acquainted with a man named Abdallah el Chahen (the poet.) Knowing that poets are sought after by the great, I asked him about all the tribes he had visited, and learned with pleasure that he had been for a long time with the Drayhy. I obtained from him all the information I had desired

One day Nasser made me write to Sheik Saddad, and him of Corietain, to demand from each a thousand piastres and six machlas. This claim is called right of fraternity: it is an arrangement between the sheiks of villages and the more powerful chiefs of the Bedouins, to be protected against the ravages of the other tribes. This is an annual tax. These unhappy villages are ruined to satisfy two tyrants—the Bedouins and the Turks.

Mehanna holds this fraternity with all the villages of the territories of Damascus, Homs, and Hama, which brings him in a revenue of about fifty thousand piastres. The pacha of Damascus pays him twelve thousand five hundred, and the cities of Homs and Hama furnish him besides a certain quantity of corn, rice, dried grapes, and stuffs. The small tribes bring him butter and cheese. In spite of all, he never has any money, and is often in debt, without having any expenses to incur; which greatly astonished us. We learned that he gave all away in presents to the most distinguished warriors, either of his own tribe or to others, and that he had thus raised for himself a powerful party. He is always ill-clothed, and when he receives a handsome pelisse or other article for a present, he gives it to the person who happens to be near him at the moment. The Bedouin proverb, that *generosity covers all defects*, is amply verified in Mehanna, whose liberality alone renders the conduct of Nasser bearable.

A short time after this event we went to encamp, three hours from the Orontes, upon lands called El Zididi, on which there are many springs.

Mehanna having one day been with ten horsemen to visit the Aga of Homs, returned loaded with presents from all the merchants, who cultivate his friendship, because, wheresoever dissatisfied with them, he intercepts their commerce and plunders the caravans.—Immediately upon his return, Nasser set forth on an expedition against the tribe Abdelli, which is commanded by the Emir El Doghiani, and encamped near Palmyra, on two small hills of equal size, called Eldain (the breast;) he returned after three days with five hundred camels and two hundred sheep. In this affair we lost three men, and Zamel's mare was killed under him. On the other hand, we took three mares, killed ten men, and wounded twenty more. Notwithstanding this success, the Bedouins were indignant at Nasser's want of faith, who had no cause of hatred against this tribe.

On all sides measures were taken with the Drayhy, to destroy the tribe El Hassnnee. The news reached the Emir Douhi, the chief of the tribe Would Ali, a kinsman and intimate friend of Mehanna, and who, as well as himself, is charged with the escort of the grand caravan; and he came with thirty horsemen to make known the danger with which he was threatened. The heads of the tribe went out to meet Douhi: having entered the tent, Mehanna ordered coffee; the emir stopped him and said, "Mehanna, thy coffee is drunk already! I come here neither to eat nor drink, but to inform thee that the behaviour of thy son Nasser Pacha (for so he styled him in derision) is bringing down destruction upon thee and thine: know that all the Bedouins have leagued together, and are about to declare against thee a war of extermination." Mehanna, changing colour, exclaimed, "Well, art thou now satisfied, Nasser? Thou wilt be the last of the race of Melkghem."

Nasser, still obstinate, replied that he should make head against all the Bedouins; and that he should have the support of twenty thousand Osmanlis, as well as that of Mola Ismael, the chief of the Kurdish cavalry, who bears the schako. Douhi passed the night in endeavouring to turn Nasser from his projects, but without succeeding: the day following, he departed, saying,

"My conscience forbids me to join you. Our relationship, and the bread we have eaten together, prevent me from declaring war against you. Farewell; I leave you with sorrow."

From this moment our time passed very disagreeably with the Bedouins. We could never quit them, for all the people who went to a distance from the tents were massacred. There were continual attacks on both sides, sudden changes of the encampment for greater security, alarms, reprisals, incessant disputes between Mehanna and his son; but the old man was so kind and so credulous, that Nasser always succeeded in persuading him that he was in the right.

We were told a thousand traits of his simplicity: amongst others, that being at Damascus whilst Yousouf Pacha, the grand vizier of the Porte, was holding his court there on his return from Egypt after the departure of the French, Mehanna was presented to him, as well as the other grandees; but, being little acquainted with Turkish etiquette, he accosted him without ceremony and with the Bedouin mode of salutation, and placed himself on the divan by his side without being invited. Yousouf, equally unaccustomed to the usages of the Bedouins, and ignorant of the dignity of the little shabby old man who treated him with such familiarity, ordered him to be taken from his presence and beheaded. The slaves took him out, and were preparing to execute the order, when the Pacha of Damascus cried aloud, "Hold! what is it you are doing? If there should fall a hair of his head, with all your power, you will never send another caravan to Mecca." The vizier instantly had him brought back, and placed him by his side; he gave him coffee, had him invested with a rich Cachemire turban, a rich gombaz (robe,) and a pelisse of honour, and presented him with a thousand piastres. Mehanna, deaf, and besides not understanding Turkish, knew nothing of what was passing; but taking off the fine clothes, he gave them to three of his slaves who accompanied him. The vizier asked him, through the dragoman, if he was not satisfied with the present. Mehanna replied, "Tell the vizier of the sultan, that we Bedouins seek not to distinguish ourselves by fine clothes: I am ill clad, but all the Bedouins know me; they know that I am Mehanna el Zadel, the son of Melkghem." The pacha, not daring to offend him, affected to smile, and to be much pleased.

The summer passed away. By the month of October the tribe was in the vicinity of Aleppo. My heart beat on finding myself so near my home; but, according to our agreement, I could not even send news of myself to my friends. Sheik Ibrahim desired to pass the winter at Damascus—no Bedouin durst conduct us. We obtained with great difficulty an escort as far as a village, two days from Aleppo, called Soghene (the hot.) The hospitable inhabitants contended for the pleasure of receiving us. A natural warm bath accounts for the name of the village; and the beauty of its inhabitants may probably be attributable to its warm springs. From thence we reached Palmyra, but with a difficulty for which we were indemnified by the pleasure of seeing Sheik Ragial again. After passing a fortnight with our friends, we went back to Corietain, where Sheik Selim and the curate Moussi welcomed us with genuine kindness;—they were never tired of hearing our accounts of the Bedouins.—Sheik Ibrahim satisfied their friendly concern about our affairs, by saying that our speculation was wonderfully advantageous; that we had gained more than we had expected; whilst in reality, between presents and losses, we only had remaining the goods deposited with Moussi.—We lost thirty days at Corietain in preparing for our departure. Winter was rapidly coming on, and no one durst furnish us with cattle, being convinced we should be plundered on the road. At last, Sheik Ibrahim bought a bad horse, I hired an ass, and in miserable weather, with a freezing wind, we set off, accompanied by four men on foot, for the village of Dair Antié. After some hours we arrived at a defile between two mountains, named Beni el Gebelain. At this spot, twenty Bedouin horsemen came upon us. Our guides, far from defending us, hid their guns and remained spectators of our disaster. The Bedouins stripped us, and left us nothing but our shirts. We implored them to kill us rather than expose us to the cold. At last, touched at our condition, they had the generosity to leave each of us a gombaz. As for our beasts, they were too sorry to tempt them. Being hardly able to walk, they would have only uselessly detained them. Night came on, and the cold was excessive, and deprived us of the use of speech. Our eyes were red, our skin blue; at the end of some time I fell to the ground, fainting and frozen. Sheik Ibrahim in despair made gesticulations to the guides, but was unable to speak. One of them, a Syrian Christian, took pity upon me and the grief of Sheik Ibrahim; he threw down his horse, which was also half dead with cold and fatigue, killed it, opened the belly, and placed me without consciousness in the skin, with only my head out. At the end of half an hour, I regained my senses, quite astonished at finding myself alive again, and in so strange a position. Warmth restored my speech; and I earnestly thanked Sheik Ibrahim and the good Arab. I took courage, and found strength to proceed. A little after, our guides cried out, "Here's the village!" and we entered the first house. It belonged to a farrier, named Hanna el Bitar. He showed a lively sympathy in our situation, set about covering us both with camel-dung, and gave us a little wine —a few drops at a time: having thus restored our strength and warmth, he withdrew us from our dunghill, put us to bed, and made us take some good soup. After a sleep, which was indispensable, we borrowed two hundred piastres to pay our guides and carry us to Damascus, which we reached the 23d December, 1810.

M. Chabassan, a French physician, the only Frank at Damascus, received us; but as we were to pass the winter here, we afterwards took up our quarters in the Lazarist Convent, which was abandoned.

I will not describe the celebrated city of Sham (Damascus), the Gate of Glory (Bab el

Cahbé), as the Turks style it. Our long residence has enabled us to know it minutely; but it has been too often visited by travellers to offer any new interest. I return to my narrative.

One day, being at the bazaar to pass away the time in the Turkish fashion, we saw running towards us a Bedouin, who embraced us, saying, " Do you not recollect your brother Hettall, who ate your bread at Nuarat el Nahaman?" Delighted with meeting him, we took him home, and having regaled him, and asked him many questions, we learned that the affairs of the tribe Hassnnee were in a bad condition, and that the league against them was extending daily. Hettall told us that he was of the tribe of Would Ali, whose chief, Douhi, was known to us. This tribe winters in the territory of Sarka and Balka; it reaches from the country of Ismael to the Dead Sea, and returns to Horan in the spring. He proposed to us to visit it, promising a good sale for our merchandise. Having consented, it was agreed that he should come for us in the month of March.

Sheik Ibrahim having received, through the intervention of M. Chabassan, a group of a thousand tallaris from Aleppo, desired me to make new purchases. When they were completed, I showed them to him, and asked whether any thing would remain for us at our return? "My dear son," he replied, "the gratitude of every chief of a tribe brings me more than all my merchandise.—Be under no concern. You also shall receive your return in money and in reputation. You shall be renowned in your time ; but I must know all the tribes and their chiefs. I depend upon you to get to the Drayhy, and for that purpose you must absolutely pass for a Bedouin. Let your beard grow, dress like them, and imitate their usages. Ask no explanations—remember our terms." My only reply was, "May God give us strength!"

Twenty times was I on the point of abandoning an enterprise of which I perceived all the dangers without knowing the object. This silence, this blind obedience, became insupportable. However, my wish to come to the issue, and my attachment to M. Lascaris, gave me patience.

At the time agreed, Hettall arrived with three camels and two guides, and we set out the 15th March, 1811, one year and twenty-eight days after our first departure from Aleppo. The tribe was at a place called Misarib, three days from Damascus. Nothing remarkable happened on the road. We passed the nights under a starry sky; and on the third day, by sunset, we were in the midst of the tents of Would Ali. The *coup d'œil* was delightful. Every tent was surrounded by horses, camels, goats, and sheep, with the lance of the horseman planted at the entrance : that of the Emir Douhi arose in the centre. He received us with all possible consideration, and made us sup with him. He is a man of understanding, and is equally loved and feared by his people. He commands five thousand tents, and three tribes, which are joined to his; those of Benin Sakhrer, of El Serhaan, and El Sarddié. He had divided his soldiers into companies or divisions, each commanded by one of his kinsmen.

The Bedouins are fond of hearing stories after supper. This is one that the emir told us: it depicts the extreme attachment they have for their horses, and the self-love they manifest with regard to their own qualities.

One of his tribe, named Giabal, possessed a very celebrated mare. Hassad Pacha, then vizier of Damascus, made him on various occasions all sorts of offers to part with it, but in vain, for a Bedouin loves his horse as he does his wife. The pacha then employed threats, but with no better success. At length, another Bedouin, named Giafar, came to the pacha, and asked what he would give him if he brought him Giabal's mare? "I will fill thy barley sack with gold," replied Hassad, who felt indignant at his want of success. This took place without transpiring; and Giabal fastened his mare at night by the foot with an iron ring, the chain of which passed into his tent, being held by a picket fixed in the ground under the very felt which served him and his wife as a bed. At midnight, Giafar creeps into the tent on all-fours, and, insinuating himself between Giabal and his wife, gently pushes first the one, and then the other: the husband thought his wife was pushing, the wife thought the same of the husband; and each made more room. Giafar then,. with a knife well sharpened, makes a slit in the felt, takes out the picket, unties the mare, mounts her, and, grasping Giabal's lance, pricks him slightly with it, calling out, "It is I, Giafar, who have taken thy noble mare; I give thee early notice!" and off he goes. Giabal instantly darts from the tent, calls his friends, mounts his brother's mare, and pursues Giafar for four hours. Giabal's brother's mare was of the same blood as his own, though not so good. Outstripping all the other horsemen, he was on the point of overtaking Giafar, when he cried out, "Pinch her right ear, and give her the stirrup." Giafar did so, and flew like lightning. The pursuit was then useless: the distance between them was too great. The other Bedouins reproached Giabal with being himself the cause of the loss of his mare.* "I would rather," said he, "lose her, than lower her reputation. Would you have me let it be said in the tribe of Would Ali, that any other mare has outrun mine? I have at least the satisfaction of saying that no other could overtake her." He returned with this consolation, and Giafar received the price of his address.

Some one else related that in the tribe of Nedgde there was a mare of equal reputation with that belonging to Giabal, and that a Bedouin of another tribe, named Daher, was almost mad with longing to possess her. Having in vain offered all his camels and his riches, he determined to stain his face with the juice of an herb, to clothe himself in rags, to tie up his

* Every Bedouin accustoms his horse to some sign when it is to put out all its speed. He employs it only on pressing occasions, and never confides the secret even to his own son.

neck and legs like a lame beggar, and, thus equipped, to wait for Nabee, the owner of the mare, in a road by which he knew he must pass. When he drew near, he said to him in a feeble voice: "I am a poor stranger: for three days I have been unable to stir from this to get food: help me, and God will reward you." The Bedouin offered to take him on his horse, and carry him home; but the rogue replied: "I am not able to rise, I have not strength." The other, full of compassion, dismounted, brought the mare close, and placed him on her with great difficulty. As soon as he found himself in the saddle, Daher gave her a touch with the stirrup, and went off, saying—"It is I, Daher, who have got her and am carrying her off."

The owner of the mare called out to him to listen: sure that he could not be pursued, he returned, and stopped at a short distance, for Nabbee was armed with his lance. He then said to him, "Thou hast my mare; since it pleases God, I wish thee success: but, I conjure thee, tell no one how thou hast obtained her." "Why not?" said Daher. "Because some one really ill might remain without aid: you would be the cause why no one would perform an act of charity more, from the fear of being duped as I have been." Struck with these words, Daher reflected a moment, dismounted from the horse and gave her back to her master, and embraced him. Nabee took him home. They remained together three days, and swore fraternity.

Sheik Ibrahim was enchanted with these stories, which gave him to understand the character and the generosity of the Bedouins. The tribe of Douhi is richer and more rapacious than that of Mehanna; their horses are finer. We stayed with them a fortnight. Sheik Ibrahim gave presents to all the chiefs, and sold some articles to the women, to keep up our character of merchants. We then went to visit the three tributary sheiks of the Emir Douhi.

Sheik Ibrahim told me that he had no other object in staying among the Bedouins than that of giving me an opportunity of studying more closely their language and their customs; that it was necessary for his own purposes to get to the Drayhy; but that I must avail myself of our roamings amidst the tribes to take exact notes of their names and their numbers, which it was most important to him to know.

Their manner of speech is extremely difficult to acquire, even for an Arab, although in fact it is the same language. I applied myself with success. I also learned, in the course of our long wanderings, the names of all the sheiks and the numbers of all the tribes, a thing which had never been accomplished before: I shall give the list at the end of my journal.

The numerous tribes are often obliged to divide themselves into detachments from two hundred to five hundred tents, and to occupy a large space, in order to procure water and pasturage for their flocks. We went successively through their encampments, until we could find means to transport ourselves to the Drayhy, who was at war with the tribes of the territory of Damascus. We were universally well received.

In one tribe it was a poor widow who showed us hospitality. In order to regale us, she killed her last sheep and borrowed bread. She informed us that her husband and her three sons had been killed in the war against the Wahabees, a formidable tribe in the neighbourhood of Mecca. Expressing our astonishment that she should rob herself on our account:—"He that enters the house of the living," said she, "and does not eat, it is as though he were visiting the dead."

One tribe already considerable had been lately formed in the following manner:—A Bedouin had a very beautiful daughter, whom the chief of his tribe demanded in marriage; but he would not give her, and in order to avoid his solicitations he went away furtively with all his family. The sheik being told of what had happened, some one said: "Serah (he is gone)." "Serhan* (he is a wolf)," replied he; meaning by that, that he was a savage. From that time the tribe of which this Bedouin became chief, has been always called the tribe El Serhan (the wolf.) Whenever the Bedouins are courageous and have good horses, they in a short time become powerful.

At last we heard of the arrival of the Drayhy in Mesopotamia. At this period Sheik Ibrahim was obliged to go to Damascus for merchandize and money, which were both equally wanting. We had made acquaintance there with a Be-

* A puh not easy to translate: *Serah* means gone; *Serhan*, wolf.

douin of one of the tribes near the Euphrates, which had preserved a neutrality in the affair of Nasser. This Bedouin, whose name was Gazens el Hamad, had come with others to Damascus to sell butter. He engaged to carry our goods on his camels, and take us to the Drayhy: but alas! we were not destined to reach him so easily. Scarcely were we come to Corietain, to take back our goods left at the depot, when we received news of a victory gained by Zaher, the son of the Drayhy, over Nasser; a victory which gave renewed violence to the war. All the tribes ranged themselves on one side or the other. That of Salkeh, our guide's tribe, had been attacked by the Drayhy, who was following up his advantages with great inveteracy, and no one dared to cross the desert. M. Lascaris was in despair. He could neither eat nor sleep: in short, exasperated to the highest degree at finding himself stopped in his projects, he even found fault with me. I then said to him,—"It is now time we should understand one another. If you wish to get to the Drayhy for the purpose of trading, it is utter madness, and I decline to follow you. If you have other projects or motives adequate to the exposure of your life, let me know them, and you shall find me ready to sacrifice myself to serve you." "Well then, my dear son!" said he, "I will trust you: know that this commerce is merely a pretence to conceal a mission with which I was charged at Paris. These are my instructions, reduced to ten heads.

1. To set out from Paris to Aleppo.
2. To find a zealous Arab, and to attach him to me as interpreter.
3. To acquire a knowledge of the language.
4. To go to Palmyra.
5. To penetrate amongst the Bedouins.
6. To become acquainted with all the chiefs, and to gain their friendship.
7. To unite them together in the same cause.
8. To induce them to break off all alliance with the Osmanlis.
9. To get acquainted with the whole desert, the halting-places, and where water and pasturage are to be found, as far even as the frontiers of India.
10. To return to Europe, safe and sound, after having accomplished my mission."

"And after that?" said I;—but he imposed silence. "Recollect our conditions," added he; "I will let you know all by degrees. At present let it suffice to know that I must reach the Drayhy, even though it should cost me my life."

This half-confidence vexed me, and prevented sleep in my turn: to find difficulties almost insurmountable, and to perceive but very confusedly the advantages of my devotion, was sufficiently disheartening. However, I took the resolution of persevering to the end, as I was so far engaged, and I dwelt only on the means of success. My beard had sprouted; I was perfectly versed in the language of the Bedouins; I resolved to go alone and on foot to the Drayhy: it was the only possible chance to be attempted.

I went to seek my friend Wardi, who had recalled me to life by putting me into his horse's belly, and communicated to him my intention. After having endeavoured to divert me from it, by telling me that the fatigue would be great; that there would be ten painful nights' march; that we must hide ourselves by day, not to be seen on the road; that we should be unable to carry with us what was strictly necessary: seeing that nothing could make me retract, he engaged to go with me as guide, in consideration of a large sum of money. Having told my resolution to M. Lascaris, he also made many friendly objections on the score of the dangers I should incur; but, in reality, I perceived that he was well pleased with me.

We settled all our matters; I agreed to write to him by the return of my guide, after having arrived at the Drayhy; and the night was far advanced when we threw ourselves on our beds. I was very much agitated; my sleep evinced it, and I soon woke M. Lascaris by my cries. I dreamt that being at the top of a steep rock, at the foot of which flowed a rapid river that I was unable to pass, I had lain down at the brink of the precipice, and that all at once a tree had taken root in my mouth; that it grew, and spread its branches like a green tent, but in growing it tore my throat, and its roots penetrated into my entrails; and I uttered violent cries. Having related my dream to Sheik Ibrahim, he was in great wonder at it, and declared that it was an excellent omen, and prognosticated after many difficulties important results.

It was essential that I should be covered with rags, in order not to excite suspicion or cupidity if we were discovered on the road. This was my costume for the journey: a coarse cotton shirt pieced; a dirty torn gombaz; an old caffié, with a bit of linen, once white, for a turban; a sheepskin cloak with half the wool off, and shoes mended to the weight of four pounds: besides these, a leather belt, from which hung a knife worth two paras, a steel, a little tobacco in an old bag, and a pipe. I blackened my eyes, and dirtied my face, and then presented myself to Sheik Ibrahim to take my leave. On seeing me, he shed tears:—" May God," said he, " give you strength enough to accomplish your generous design! I shall owe every thing to your perseverance. May the Almighty be with you and preserve you from all danger! may he blind the wicked, and bring you back that I may reward you!" I could hardly refrain from tears in my turn. At last, however, the conversation becoming more cheerful, Sheik Ibrahim said smilingly, that if I were to go to Paris in this costume, I should get much money by showing myself.—We supped; and at sunset we departed. I walked without fatigue till midnight: but then my feet began to swell. My shoes hurt me, and I took them off; the thorns of the plants the camels browse on pricked me, and the small stones wounded me. I tried to put on my shoes; and in continual suffering I walked on till morning. A little grotto gave us shelter for the day. I wrapped my feet in a piece of my cloak that I tore off, and slept without having strength to take any nourishment. I was still asleep when my guide called me to depart: my feet were much swollen—my heart failed me—I wished to wait till the following day. My conductor reproached me for my weaknes:—"I knew well enough," said he, "that you were too delicate for such a journey. I before told you that it was impossible to stop here: if we pass the night, we must also pass the next day; our provisions will be consumed, and we shall die of hunger in the desert. We had better give up our undertaking while there is yet time."

These words reanimated me, and we set off. I dragged myself along with difficulty till near midnight, when we came to a plain, in which the sand rose and fell in undulations: here we rested ourselves till day. The first dawn enabled us to perceive at a distance two objects, which we took for camels. My guide, alarmed, dug a hole in the sand, to conceal us; we got in up to the neck, leaving only our heads out. In this painful situation we remained with our eyes fixed on the supposed camels, when, about noon, Wardi exclaimed, "God be praised! they are only ostriches." We got out of our grave with joy, and for the first time since our departure I ate a little cake and drank a drop of water. We remained there till night, awaiting the time to move forward. Being then in the midst of the sands, I suffered less in walking. We passed the next day in sleeping. We were opposite Palmyra, to the south. Daybreak, after the fourth night, overtook us at the bank of a large river called El Rahib, running from south to north; my guide stripped, and carried me on his back to the other side, and then returned for his clothes. I wished to rest myself, but he told me it would not be prudent to stop where the river was fordable. In fact, we had not proceeded half an hour, when we saw five hundred well-mounted Bedouins approaching the river, going from the east to the west. Having found some low bushes, we halted amongst them till night. The sixth night brought us within some hours of the Euphrates. The seventh day, the great difficulty was over; and if I had not suffered so much in my feet, I could have forgotten all my fatigues at the sight of the sunrise on the banks of that magnificent river. Some hospitable Bedouins, whose occupation it is to take people over from one side to the other, took us into their tents, where for the first time we made a hearty meal. We obtained intelligence respecting the Drayhy: he was at three days' distance between Zaite and Zauer. He had made peace with the Emir Fahed, imposing tribute on him; they spoke to me of his military talents and his extreme courage, of his intention to annihilate Mehanna and Nasser, and to return to his desert near Bassora and Bagdad. These details were just as I was wishing: I took my resolution immediately. I asked for a guide to take me to the Drayhy, telling the Bedouins that I was a merchant of Aleppo, having a correspondent at Bagdad, who owed me twenty-five thousand piastres, and who had just become bankrupt: that the war between the Bedouins had intercepted the communications, and I had no other resource than to risk myself alone, and put myself under the protection of the Drayhy to get to Bagdad, where all my fortune was at stake. These kind Bedouins offered vows to Allah that I might recover my money; and Wardi himself took more interest in my journey, when he understood its importance. After having passed the day in examining the tribe Beni Tay, we departed the next day well escorted; and nothing interesting occurred on our march. We saw the setting sun of the third day gild the five thousand tents of the Drayhy, which covered the plain as far as the eye could reach. Surrounded by camels, horses, and flocks, which concealed the earth, never had I seen such a spectacle of power and wealth. The emir's tent in the centre was a hundred and sixty feet long. He received me very politely, and without any question proposed to me to sup with him. After supper, he said to me: "Whence do you come, and whither are you going?" I replied as I had done to the Bedouins of the Euphrates. "You are welcome, then," said he; "your arrival will cause a thousand benedictions. Please God you will succeed; but, according to our custom, we cannot speak of business till after three days devoted to hospitality and repose." I made the customary thanks, and retired. The next day I despatched Wardi to M. Lascaris.

The Drayhy is a man of fifty, tall, and of a handsome countenance, with a small beard entirely white; his aspect is stern; he is considered as the most able of all the chiefs of tribes; he has two sons, Zaer and Sahdoun: they are married, and dwell in the same tent as himself. His tribe, called El Dualla, is numerous and very rich. Chance favoured me wonderfully from the first day of my arrival. The emir was in want of a secretary; I offered to assist him for the moment, and I soon gained his confidence by the hints and the information I was able to give him regarding the tribes I had studied. When I spoke to him of my own business, he expressed so much regret at seeing me about to depart, that I feigned to yield to his wishes. He said, "If you will remain with me, you shall be like my son; all that you say shall be done." I availed myself of this confidence, to induce him to pass over the Euphrates, in order to bring him nearer to Sheik Ibrahim: I suggested to him all the influence he might gain over the tribes of the country, by withdrawing them from Nasser: I represented to him all the presents they would be obliged to offer him; the terror with which he would inspire the Osmanlis, and the mischief he would do his enemies by consuming their pasturage. As it was the first time he was quitting the desert of Bagdad to come into Mesopotamia, my advice and my information were a great resource to him, and he followed them. The departure was superb to witness. The horsemen before, on horses of high pedigree; women on howdahs magnificently draped, and on dromedaries, surrounded by negress slaves. Men, loaded with provisions, were running throughout the caravan, calling out: "Who is hungry?" and distributing bread, dates, &c. Every three hours, a halt was made, to take coffee; and at night the tents were raised as if by enchantment. We followed the banks of the Euphrates, whose clear waters gleamed like silver: I myself was mounted on a mare of pure blood; and the whole journey appeared like a triumphal march, presenting a strong contrast with my former passage over the same country, in my rags and with my tortured feet.

On the fourth day, the Emir Zahed met us with a thousand horse. All sorts of sports ensued on horseback and with lance. At night, the Drayhy, his sons, and myself, went to sup in the tribe of Zahed. The day following, we crossed the river, encamped on the Damascus territory, and kept advancing westward. We then encamped at El Jaffet, in the pachalik of Aleppo. The report of the arrival of the Drayhy was quickly spread, and he received from Mehanna a letter beginning with their respective titles, and continuing thus:

"In the name of God most merciful, health! We have learnt with surprise that you have passed the Euphrates, and are advancing into the provinces left us by our fathers. Do you then think that you alone can devour the pasture of all the birds? Know that we have so many warriors that we are unable to number them. Besides, we shall be supported by the valiant Osmanlis, whom nothing can resist: we counsel you to return by the road by which you came; otherwise all conceivable misfortunes will befall you, and repentance will come too late."

On reading this letter, I saw the Drayhy growing pale with anger; his eyes flashed fire.

After a momentary silence, "Katib," said he, in a terrible voice, "take your pen, and write to this dog!"

This was the answer:—"I have read your menaces, which with me do not weigh a grain of mustard. I shall lower your flag, and purify the earth from you and your renegade of a son, Nasser. As for the territory you claim, the sword shall decide it. Soon will I set forward to exterminate you. Prepare yourself. War is declared."

Then addressing myself to the Drayhy: "I have some advice to give you," said I. "You are a stranger here; you know not which party the tribes of the country will espouse. Mehanna is loved by the Bedouins, and supported by the Turks; you are about to undertake a war, without knowing the number of your enemies. If you experience a single defeat, all will combine against you, and you will not be strong enough to resist. Send then a message to the neighbouring sheiks to tell them that you are come to destroy the tents of Melkghem, in order to free them from the yoke of the Osmanlis; and demand of them to declare themselves. Thus, being aware of your force, you may compare it with theirs, and act in consequence."—"You are truly a man of sage counsel," said the Drayhy, delighted with my suggestion. "I am nothing of myself," I replied: "it is by the favour of my master, if I know any thing: it is he who is the man of wisdom and knowledge, and well skilled in affairs: he alone is capable of giving you advice. You

would be enchanted with him, if you could know him. I am sure that if you had him with you, and were aided by his sagacity, you would become chief of all the Bedouins of the desert."
"I will instantly send a hundred horsemen to bring him," said the Drayhy, with alacrity. "We are still too far off," said I; "the journey would be painful; when we get nearer to Corietain I will bring him to you."

I was fearful of some untoward accident to the Sheik Ibrahim; and wished to be near him, to present him myself. I was so attached to him, that I could have sacrificed myself a thousand times to do him service.

But to return to our council of war. The Drayhy gave me a list, to write to ten of the principal sheiks of the tribes. This was his letter:

"I have left my country to come and deliver you from the tyranny of Nasser, who wishes to become your master by the power of the Turks; to change your usages, destroy your manners, and subject you to the Osmanlis. I have declared war against him; tell me frankly if you are for him or for me; and let those who will aid me come and join me.—Health!"

The next day, having despatched ten horsemen with these letters, we advanced into the extensive and beautiful territory of Chaumerie, thirty hours from Hama. After a short absence, our messengers returned. The Emir Douhi, and the Sheik Sellame, answered that they should preserve a neutrality; Sheik Cassem, the kinsman of Mehanna, declared for him; the remaining seven tribes came and encamped around us, their sheiks promising the Drayhy to partake his dangers for life or for death. However, our spies brought intelligence that Mehanna in alarm had sent Nasser to Hama to obtain assistance from the Turks. The Drayhy immediately assembled his army, eight thousand strong, six thousand horse, and a thousand deloulmardoufs,—that is to say, a thousand camels, each carrying two men armed with matchlocks,—and began to march on the fourth day; leaving orders for the rest of the tribe to follow the second day after, in order the more to stimulate the courage of his warriors in the battle, by the vicinity of their wives and children. I remained with the latter, and we went to encamp at El Jamié, one hour from the tribe El Hassnnée, and two days from Hama. On the fifth day, the Drayhy announced to us a brilliant victory; and shortly afterwards arrived the camels, sheep, horses and arms, taken from the enemy. The men, who had been obliged to remain at the tents in charge of the baggage, went out to meet the conquerors, and demand their share of the spoil, to which they are entitled; and the army soon appeared in triumph.

The Drayhy had taken Mehanna rather by surprise, during the absence of Nasser; but the tribe of Hassnnée having shouted their warcry, the combatants proved nearly equal in numbers; the battle lasted till night. Our warriors lost twenty-two men; but they killed twice as many of the enemy, and took possession of their flocks. Zaher also took the mare of Fares, the son of Mehanna, which amongst the Bedouins is reckoned a glorious exploit.

After his defeat, Mehanna crossed the Orontes at the north of Hama, and encamped near Homs, to await the Osmanlis and return with them to take his revenge. In fact, on the fifth day, the shepherds ran crying that the Turks headed by Nasser were taking possession of the flocks. Immediately our warriors flew in pursuit, and overtook them, when a more terrible battle than the first was fought, during which the enemy drove off a great part of our cattle towards his camp. The advantage remained with our men, who carried off a considerable spoil from the Turks; but the loss of our flocks was considerable. We had to regret the loss of only twelve men, but amongst them was the nephew of the Drayhy, Ali, whose death was universally lamented. His uncle remained three days without eating; and swore by Almighty God that he would kill Nasser, to revenge the death of Ali.

Attacks were taking place every day; the Osmanlis of Damascus, Homs, and Hama were in a state of consternation, and attempted to collect together the Arabs of Horam and Idumea. Several tribes of the desert arrived, some to reinforce the Drayhy, others Mehanna. No caravan could pass from one city to another; the advantages were almost all on the side of the Drayhy. One day, by a singular coincidence, Fares took from us a hundred and twenty camels that were pasturing two leagues from the tents; while at the same instant Zaher carried off the like number of theirs. This simultaneous movement prevented either the one or the other from being pursued. They also had time to secure their capture. But this war of reprisals of cattle and plunder was about to assume a character of ferocity and extermination. The signal for it was given by the Dallati Turks, under the conduct of Nasser, who, having taken from the tribe of Beni Kraleb two women and a girl, carried them to the village of Zany-el-Abedin. Nasser gave the women to the soldiers; and assigned to the aga the young girl, who in the middle of the night revenged her honour by poniarding the Turk in his sleep. Her vigorous arm pierced his heart and left him dead; and then escaping without noise, she rejoined her tribe, and spread indignation and rage among the Bedouins, who swore to die or slay Nasser, and to fill vessels with his blood, to distribute among the tribes as a memorial of their vengeance.

This penalty was not long postponed; an engagement having taken place between a party commanded by Zaher, and another under the orders of Nasser, the two chiefs, whose hatred was mutual, sought each other out, and fought together with fury. The Bedouins remained spectators of the battle between these warriors, equal in valour and skill. The contest was long and terrible: at length their tired horses no longer able promptly to obey the motions of their riders, Nasser received the thrust of Zaher's lance, which pierced him through and through: he fell; his men ran away, or gave up their horses:* Zaher cut the body of Nasser to pieces, put it in a couffe (wicker basket), and sent it to Mehanna's camp by a prisoner, whose nose he cut off. He then returned to his tribe exulting in his revenge.

Mehanna sent to ask aid of the Bedouins of Chamma, of Neggde, and of the Wahabees: they promised to come to his support the following year, the time being then come for their return to the East. As we were encamped very near Corietain, I proposed to go and fetch Sheik Ibrahim. The Drayhy accepted my offer with eagerness, and gave me a strong escort. I cannot describe the happiness I felt at again seeing M. Lascaris, who received me with great warmth of heart;—as for me, I embraced him as my father, for I had never known mine, who died in my early infancy. I spent the night in relating to him all that had passed. The next day, taking leave of our friends, the curate Moussi and Sheik Selim, I took away Sheik Ibrahim, who was received with the highest distinction by the Drayhy. A grand feast of camel's flesh was prepared, which I found less disagreeable than the first time, for I was beginning to be accustomed to the food of the Bedouins. The camels intended for killing are as white as snow, and are never either worked or fatigued; the meat is red and very fat. The female gives great abundance of milk; the Bedouins drink it continually, and give the rest to their horses of pedigree, which greatly

* When a Bedouin voluntarily gives up his horse to his adversary, he may neither kill him nor make him prisoner.

strengthens them : in this way they consume all the milk, as it is not suited to make into butter. We came at last to think the taste preferable to that of goat's or sheep's milk.

An attack of the Wahabees a short time after the arrival of M. Lascaris cost the Drayhy some horsemen and much cattle. The next day Sheik Ibrahim took me aside and said, "I am pleased with the Drayhy; he is just the man I want; but it is indispensable that he should become the chief of all the Bedouins from Aleppo to the frontiers of India. It is to you I look to arrange the matter, by friendship, by threats, or by artifice; this must be effected." "You are imposing a difficult undertaking," I replied. "Every tribe has its chief; they are enemies of dependence, and never have they submitted to any yoke. I fear, if you should engage in any such project, that something disastrous will happen to you." "Still it must absolutely be done," replied M. Lascaris; "exert all your capacity; without that we shall not succeed."

I reflected a long time upon the best means of setting about the business. The first point was to inspire the Bedouins with a high idea of Sheik Ibrahim; and to effect this, as they are superstitious and credulous to excess, we got up a few chemical experiments with phosphorus and fulminating powder, hoping to astonish them. Accordingly, at night, when the chiefs of the tribe were met together under the tent of the Drayhy, Sheik Ibrahim, with a majestic air and admirable dexterity, produced effects that struck them with surprise and amazement. From that moment he appeared to them a sorcerer, a magician, or rather a divinity.

The next day the Drayhy called me and said, "Oh, Abdallah! your master is a god!" "No," replied I, "but rather a prophet; what you witnessed yesterday is nothing compared to the power he has acquired by his profound science; he is the remarkable man of the age. Learn that, if he would, he is capable of making you king of all the Bedouins: he discerned that the comet which appeared some time ago was your star, that is, is superior to that of the other Arabs, and that if you will follow his advice in every point, you will become all-powerful." This idea pleased him extremely. The desire of command and of glory sprang up with violence in his breast; and, by a coincidence truly extraordinary, I had divined the object of his superstition, for he exclaimed, "Oh, Abdallah, I see that you speak truth, and that your master is really a prophet. I had a dream some time ago, in which some fire, separating from a comet, fell upon my tent and consumed it, and I took this fire in my hand and it did not burn me. That comet surely was my star." He then called his wife, and begged her to relate herself the dream as he had told it her on awaking. I availed myself of the circumstance to confirm still more effectually the superiority of Sheik Ibrahim, and the Drayhy promised me to follow all his advice for the future. M. Lascaris, delighted at this fortunate commencement, selected from his goods a handsome present, to give to the Drayhy, who accepted it with the greatest pleasure, and perceived in it a proof that it was not to enrich ourselves that we were endeavouring to counsel him. From that time he made us eat with his wife and daughters-in-law, in the interior of their tent, instead of eating with strangers in the rabha. His wife, a descendant of a great family, and sister of a minister of Ebn Sihoud, is named Sugar: she enjoys a high reputation for courage and generosity.

Whilst we were establishing our influence over the Drayhy, a minor enemy was working in the shade to destroy our hopes and ruin us. There is in every tribe a pedler, who sells to the women various articles he brings from Damascus. The one belonging to our tribe, whose name was Absi, filled besides the office of scribe to the Drayhy; but ever since our arrival he had lost both his office and his custom. He naturally felt a great antipathy for us, and sought every possible means to calumniate us before the Bedouins, beginning with the women, whom he persuaded that we were magicians; that we wanted to carry off their daughters into a far country, and throw a spell round the women that they might have no more children; that thus the race of the Bedouins would become extinct, and that Frank conquerors would come and take possession of the country. We soon felt the effects of his calumnies, without knowing their cause. The girls fled at our approach; the women called us opprobrious names; the elderly ones even threatened us. Amongst an ignorant and credulous people, where the women possess great influence, such a danger might have become serious. At last we found out these intrigues of Absi, and acquainted the Drayhy with them, who would have put him to death on the spot. We had great difficulty in getting him only dismissed from the tribe, which in fact only gave him further opportunity to extend his malice. A village called Mohadan, hitherto tributary to Mehanna, had become so to the Drayhy since his victories. This chief having demanded a thousand piastres that were due to him, the inhabitants, at the instigation of Absi, maltreated the Emir's messenger, who punished them by carrying off their flocks. Absi persuaded the village chiefs to come with him to Damascus, and declare to the Capidji Bashi that two Frank spies had gained the confidence of the Drayhy, had made him commit all kinds of injustice, and were endeavouring to make him withdraw the Bedouins from their alliance with the Osmanlis. This denunciation was made before the Vizier Solyman Pacha, who sent a chokedar to the Drayhy, with a threatening letter, concluding with ordering him to deliver up the two infidels to his officer, that they might be led in chains to Damascus, where their public execution would operate as an example.

The Drayhy, enraged at the insolence of this letter, said to the Mussulman officer, "By Him who has raised the heavens, and lowered the earth, if thou wert not beneath my tent, I would cut off thy head, and tie it to my horse's tail; and thus should he bear my answer to your vizier. As to the two strangers who are with me, I shall never deliver them up while I live. If he wants them, let him come and take them by the power of his sword!"

I then took the Drayhy aside, and entreated him to compose himself, and leave it to me to settle the affair.

I knew that M. Lascaris was intimately connected with Solyman Pacha, and that a letter from him would produce an effect that the Drayhy little expected. M. Lascaris, whilst with the French expedition in Egypt, had married a Georgian, brought with the women of Murad Bey, who proved to be cousin to Solyman Pacha. Subsequently he had occasion to go to Acre; his wife made known her relationship to the pacha, and was loaded by him with kindness and presents, as well as her husband.

M. Lascaris therefore wrote to Solyman Pacha, informing him that the pretended spies were no other than himself and his dragoman, Fatalla Sayeghir; that all that had been said against the Drayhy was false; that it was, on the contrary, for the interest of the Porte to cultivate his friendship, and to favour his preponderance over the other Bedouins. The chokedar, who was trembling for his life, hastened to bear the letter to Damascus, and returned in two days with a most friendly answer to Sheik Ibrahim, and another for the Drayhy, of which these are the contents.—After many compliments to the emir, he adds: "We have received a letter from our dear friend, the great Sheik Ibrahim, which destroys the çalumnies of your enemies, and gives most satisfactory testimony regarding you. Your wisdom is made known to us. Henceforward we authorize you to command in the desert, according to your good pleasure. From us you shall receive only acts of friendship. We rate you above your equals. We commend to you our well-beloved Sheik Ibrahim, and Abdallah: their satisfaction will increase our regard for you," &c. The Drayhy and other chiefs were greatly astonished at the great credit of Sheik Ibrahim with the pacha. This incident crowned their consideration towards us.

I have said that the Drayhy was surnamed the Exterminater of the Turks; I inquired the origin of this epithet. This is what Sheik Abdallah told me. The Drayhy having once plundered a caravan that was going from Damascus to Bagdad, the pacha was extremely enraged; but not daring openly to avenge himself, dissembled, according to the practice of the Turks, and induced him by fair promises to come to Bagdad. The Drayhy, frank and loyal, suspected no treachery, and went to the pacha with his ordinary train of ten horsemen. He was immediately seized, bound, thrown into a dungeon, and threatened with the loss of his head, if he did not pay for his ransom a thousand purses, (a million piastres,) five thousand sheep, twenty mares of the kahillan breed, and twenty dromedaries. The Drayhy, leaving his son as hostage, went to raise this enormous ransom; and as soon as he had discharged it, he resolved on taking his revenge. The caravans and the villages were plundered; and Bagdad was itself blockaded. The pacha, having collected his troops, came out with an army of thirty thousand men and some pieces of cannon against the Drayhy, who, supported by the allied tribes, gave him battle, which lasted three days; but finding that he was gaining no decisive advantage, retired silently in the night, turned the pacha's army. and placing himself between it and Bagdad, attacked it unexpectedly on several points at the same time. Surprised by night, and on the quarter which was without defence, a panic seized the enemy's camp. The confusion became general among the Osmanlis; and the Drayhy made a great slaughter of them, remaining master of an immense booty. The pacha escaped alone and with difficulty, and shut himself up in Bagdad. This exploit spread such terror among the inhabitants, that even after the peace, his name continued an object of dread. Abdallah recounted many other achievements of the Drayhy, and ended with saying that he loved grandeur and difficulties, and wished to subject all to his dominion.

These were precisely the qualities that Sheik Ibrahim desired to find in him: he therefore devoted himself more and more to the project of making him master of all the other tribes; but the Wahabees were formidable adversaries, who a few days afterwards fell upon the tribe Would Ali, and spread themselves over the desert to force the Bedouins to pay them a tenth. Alarmed at the approach of these terrible warriors, many tribes were about to submit, when Sheik Ibrahim persuaded the Drayhy that it was for his own honour to take the field, and declare himself protector of the oppressed.

Encouraged by his example, all the tribes, with the exception of that of El Hassnnée, and Beni Sakhrer, made alliance with him to resist the Wahabees. The Drayhy marched with an army of five thousand horse, and two thousand mardouffs. We were ten days without receiving any intelligence. The anxiety in the camp was excessive; symptoms of dissatisfaction against us were becoming apparent, for being the instigators of the perilous expedition; our lives might possibly have paid the penalty of our temerity, if the uncertainty had lasted much longer. On the next day, at noon, a horseman arrived at full speed, waving his white belt at the end of his lance, and shouting aloud, "God has given us the victory!" Sheik Ibrahim gave magnificent presents to the bearer of this good news, which relieved the tribe from serious alarm, and ourselves from no small peril. Shouting and dancing round lighted fires, cattle slain, and preparations for a festival to welcome the warriors, set the camp in an unusual agitation; and all this active arrangement executed by the women, presented a most original spectacle. At night, all the camp went forth to meet the victorious army, the dust they raised being seen in the distance. As soon as we met, the cries were redoubled. Jousting, racing, firing, and all possible demonstrations of joy, accompanied us back to the camp. After our repast we obtained a recital of the exploits of the warriors.

The Wahabees were commanded by a doughty negro, a half-savage, whose name was Abu-Nocta. When he prepares for battle, he takes off his turban and boots, draws up his sleeves to his shoulders, and leaves his body almost naked, which is of prodigious size and muscular strength. His head and chin, never being shaved, are overshadowed by a bushy head of hair and black beard, which cover his entire face, his eyes gleaming beneath the shade. His whole body, too, is hairy, and affords a sight as strange as it is frightful. The Drayhy came up to him three days from Palmyra, at a spot called Heroualma. The battle was most obstinate on both sides, but ended in the flight of Abu-Nocta, who removed to the country of Neggde, leaving two hundred slain on the field of battle. The Drayhy searched out among the spoils all that had been taken from the tribe Would Ali, and restored it. This act of generosity still further attached to him the affection of the other tribes, who were coming daily to put themselves under his protection. The report of this victory gained over the terrible Abu-Nocta was disseminated everywhere. Solyman Pacha sent the conqueror a pelisse of honour, and a magnificent sabre, with his congratulations. Soon after this exploit we encamped on the frontiers of Horan.

One day, a Turkish mollah arrived at the Drayhy's; he wore the large green turban that distinguishes the descendants of Mahomet, a white flowing robe, his eyes blackened, and an enormous beard; he wore also several rows of chaplets, and an inkstand in the form of a dagger at his belt. He rode on an ass, and carried in his hand an arrow. He was come to instil his fanaticism into the Bedouins, and excite in them a great zeal for the religion of the Prophet, in order to attach them to the cause of the Turks. The Bedouins are of great simplicity of character, and remarkable for their frankness. They do not understand differences of religion, and do not willingly allow them to be spoken of. They are deists; they invoke the protection of God in all the events of life, and refer to him their success or their failures with humble resignation; but they have no ceremonies or obligatory ritual, and make no distinction between the sects of Omar and of Ali, which divide the East. They never inquired what was our religion. We told them that we were Christians; their answer was, "All men are equal in the sight of God, and are his creatures; we have no right to inquire what is the creed of other men." This discretion on their part was much more favourable to our projects than the fanaticism of the Turks; so that the arrival of the mollah gave some anxiety to Sheik Ibrahim, who went to the tent of the Drayhy, where he found the conference already begun, or rather the preaching, to which the chiefs were listening with a dissatisfied air. As they all arose at our entrance to salute us, the mollah inquired who we were, and having learnt that we were Christians:—"It is forbidden," said he, "by the laws of God, to rise before infidels; you will be cursed for holding intercourse with them; your wives will be illegitimate, and your children bastards. Such is the decree of our lord, Mahomet, whose name be for ever venerated!"

The Drayhy, without waiting for the end of his speech, got up in a rage, seized him by the beard, threw him down, and drew his sabre; Sheik Ibrahim sprang forward, withheld his arm, and conjured him to moderate his anger: at length, the emir consented to cut off his beard instead of his head, and drove him away with ignominy.

The Drayhy having attacked the tribe of Beni-Sakhrer, the only one which still opposed him, beat it completely.

However, as the autumn was now come, we commenced our return towards the east. As we approached Homs, the governor sent the Drayhy forty camels loaded with corn, ten machlas, and a pelisse of honour. Sheik Ibrahim addressed me in private and said, "We are going into the desert; we have exhausted all our stock; what must we do?" "Give me your orders," I replied; " I will go secretly to Aleppo, and get what we want, and I will engage not to make myself known to my family." It was agreed that I should rejoin the tribe at Zour; and I went to Aleppo. I took up my station in a khan but little frequented, and remote from all my acquaintances. I sent a stranger to the correspondent of M. Lascaris to get five hundred tallaris. The precaution was unnecessary, for with my long beard, my costume, and my Bedouin accent, I ran no risk of being known; I proved this sufficiently on purchasing some goods at the Bazaar. I met many of my friends there, and amused myself with behaving rudely to them. But to these moments of careless gaiety, painful ones succeeded; I passed and repassed continually before the door of my house, hoping to get a glimpse of my brother or my poor mother. My desire of seeing her above all was so great that I was twenty times on the point of breaking my word; but the conviction that she would not again allow me to return to M. Lascaris restored my courage, and after six days I was obliged to tear myself away from Aleppo, without obtaining any news of my relatives.

I overtook the tribe on the banks of the Euphrates opposite Daival-Chahar, where there are still some fine ruins of an ancient city. I found the Bedouins engaged, before crossing the river, in selling cattle, or changing them for goods with the pedlers from Aleppo. They have no idea of the value of fictitious money; they will not receive gold in payment, recognising nothing but silver tallaris. They would rather pay too much, or not receive enough in change, than admit of fractions. The merchants, aware of this foible, dexterously profit by it. Besides the exchanges, the tribes sold to the amount of twenty-five thousand tallaris; and every man put his money into his sack of flour, that it might not sound on loading and unloading.

A tragical accident happened at the passage of the Euphrates. A woman and two children, mounted on a camel, were carried down by the current before it was possible to give them any assistance. We found Mesopotamia covered with the tribes of Bagdad and Bassora. Their chiefs came daily to congratulate the Drayhy on his victory, and to make acquaintance with us, for the renown of Sheik Ibrahim had reached them. They felt indebted to him for having counselled the war against the Wahabees, whose rapacity and exactions were become intolerable. Their king, Ebn-Sihoud, was accustomed to send a mezakie to count the flocks of each individual, and to take the tenth, always choosing the best: he then had the tents taken down, from that of the sheik to that of the poorest wretch, to find his money, of which they also exacted a tenth. He was still more odious to the Bedouins, because in his extreme fanaticism, he exacted ablutions and prayers five times a day, and punished with death those who refused to submit. When he forced a tribe to make war for him, instead of sharing the gains and the losses, he kept all the plunder, and only left his allies to bewail their dead. And thus, by degrees, the Bedouins were becoming the slaves of the Wahabees, for want of a chief capable of making head against Ebn-Sihoud.

We encamped at a spot called Nain-el-Raz, three days from the Euphrates. Here the Emir Fares el Harba, the chief of the tribe El Harba, of the territory of Bassora, came to make an offensive and defensive alliance with the Drayhy. When the chiefs have to discuss any important affair, they quit the camp and hold their conference at a distance; this is called *dahra*,— secret assembly. Sheik Ibrahim having been called to the dahra, showed some mistrust of Fares, fearing that he was a spy of the Wahabees. The Drayhy said to him, "You judge of the Bedouins by the Osmanlis: know that the characters of the two people are directly opposed—treason is unknown among us." After this declaration, all the sheiks present at the council mutually pledged their word. Sheik Ibrahim took advantage of this disposition to propose to them to conclude a treaty in writing, to be signed and sealed by all those who would successively enter into the alliance against Ebn-Sihoud. This was a great step in the interest of Sheik Ibrahim, and I drew up the treaty in the following terms:—

"In the name of the God of mercy, who by his might will help us against traitors. We praise him for all his goodness, and return thanks to him for having given us to distinguish good from evil—to love liberty and to hate slavery; we acknowledge that he is the only and Almighty God, alone to be adored.

"We declare that we are confederated by our own free will without any constraint, that we are all sound in body and mind, and that we have unanimously resolved to follow the advice of Sheik Ibrahim and Abdallah el Katib, for the interest of our prosperity, of our glory, and of our liberty. The articles of our treaty are:—

"1st. To separate ourselves from the Osmanlis.

"2d. To wage a war of extirpation against the Wahabees.

"3d. Never to speak upon the subject of religion.

" 4th. To obey the orders of our brother, the great Drayhy, Ebn Chahllan.

" 5th. To oblige each sheik to answer for his tribe and to keep this engagement secret.

" 6th. To combine against those tribes who should not subscribe to it.

" 7th. To march to the assistance of those who sign the present treaty, and to combine against their enemies.

" 8th. To punish with death those who should break this alliance.

" 9th. To listen to no calumnies against Sheik Ibrahim and Abdallah.

" We the undersigned accept all the articles of this treaty; we will maintain them in the name of God and of his prophets Mahomet and Ali; declaring by these presents that we are determined to live and die in this holy alliance.

"Dated, signed, and sealed, the 12th of November, 1811."

All who were present approved and signed it.

Some time afterwards, being encamped in the large and fine plain of El Rané, the Drayhy sent couriers to the other tribes, to invite them to sign this treaty. Several chiefs set their seals to it, and those who had no seal fixed on it the impression of their finger. Among these chiefs I noticed a young man who from the age of fifteen had governed the tribe of El Ollama, which bears a character very superior to those of the other Bedouins. They cultivate poetry, are well informed, and in general very eloquent. This young sheik thus related the origin of his tribe:—

A Bedouin of Bagdad was held in high reputation for sagacity. A man one day came to him, saying:—"My wife disappeared four days ago; I have sought her ever since in vain: I have three weeping children, and I am in despair; assist me with your advice." Aliaony consoled the unfortunate man, recommended him to stay with his children, and promised him to seek his wife for him, and bring her back dead or alive. In collecting all sorts of intelligence upon the subject, he learnt that the woman was remarkably beautiful; he himself had a libertine son, who had also been some days absent: a ray of light broke upon his mind—he mounted his dromedary and searched the desert. He perceived from afar an assemblage of eagles, hastened towards them, and found at the entrance of a grotto the dead body of a woman. Examining the spot, he discovered the track of a camel, and part of the trimming of a wallet: he brought away this dumb witness and retraced his steps. On returning to his tent, he found his son arrived: his torn wallet wanted the fatal trimming. Overwhelmed by his father's reproaches, the young man confessed his crime: Aliaony cut off his head, sent for the husband, and said to him:—"My son killed your wife—I have punished him and revenged you; I have a daughter, and give her to you in marriage." This trait of barbarous justice enhanced the reputation of Aliaony: he was elected chief of his tribe, which from his name assumed that of El Ollama, signifying wise,—an appellation which the tribe has always justified.

As we approached Bagdad, our treaty daily received a number of additional signatures.

After quitting El Rané, we encamped at Ain el Oussada, near the river El Cabour. During our sojourn there, a courier despatched by the Drayhy to the Sheik Giandal, chief of the tribe of Wualdi, having been very ill received, returned, bearing an offensive message to the Drayhy. His sons were desirous of taking immediate vengeance. Sheik Ibrahim opposed them, representing that it was always time enough to make war, and that it was right first to try persuasion. I proposed to the emir to go myself with explanations to Giandal. At first he refused the offer, saying:—"Why should you take the trouble of going to him? Let him come himself, or my sabre shall compel him." He yielded, however, at length to my arguments, and I set out escorted by two Bedouins. Giandal received me with anger, and learning who I was, said to me:—"If I had met you anywhere but under my tent, you should never have eaten bread again: be thankful to our customs, which forbid my killing you."
—"Words do not kill," said I; "I am your friend, and have your good at heart. I am come to ask a private interview with you. If what I have to say to you does not satisfy you, I shall return by the way that I came." Seeing my *sang-froid*, he stood up, called his eldest son, conducted me beyond the tents, where we sat down upon the ground, and I thus opened the conference:—

"Which do you prefer, slavery or liberty?"
"Liberty, undoubtedly!"

" Union or discord?"—" Union!"
"Greatness or abasement?"—" Greatness!"
" Poverty or riches?"—" Riches!"
" Good or evil?"—" Good!"

" All these advantages we are desirous of securing to you: we wish to release you from slavery to the Wahabees, and from the tyranny of the Osmanlis, by a general confederation which shall make us powerful and free. " Why do you refuse to join us?" He answered: " What you say is plausible, but we shall never be strong enough to resist Ebn Sihoud!"—" Ebn Sihoud is a man like yourself; he is moreover a tyrant, and God does not favour oppressors: it is not numbers, but intelligence which gives the superiority; power does not rest in the sabre which strikes, but in the will which directs it." The conference lasted some time longer; but in the end I convinced him, and persuaded him to accompany me to the Drayhy, who was highly satisfied with the issue of my negotiation.

We next encamped near the mountains of Sangiar, which are inhabited by the worshippers of an evil spirit. The principal tribe of the country, commanded by Hammond el Tammer, is fixed near the river Sagiour, and does not wander like the others. Hammond refused at first to enter into the alliance. I had a long correspondence with him on this subject, and having at length persuaded him to join us, great rejoicings took place on both sides. Hammond invited the Drayhy to visit him, and received him magnificently. Five camels and thirty sheep were slaughtered for the entertainment, which was served on the ground without the tents. Large dishes of tinned copper, resembling silver, were borne each by four men, containing a mountain of rice six feet high, surmounted by an entire sheep or the quarter of a camel. In other dishes not so large, was a roast sheep or a camel's ham; and a multitude of little dishes, filled with dates and other dried fruits, were distributed in the intervals. Their bread is excellent. They bring their corn from Diabekir, and their rice from Marhach and Mallatia. When we were seated, or rather squatted, round this feast, we could not distinguish the persons opposite to us. The Bedouins of this tribe dress much more richly than the others: the women are very pretty; they wear silk dresses, many bracelets and ear-rings of gold and silver, and a golden ring in the nose.

After some days passed in festivities, we continued our journey and approached a river, or rather an arm of the Euphrates, which connects it with the Tigris. Here we were joined by a courier, who in five days had travelled on a dromedary a distance which takes thirty at the pace of a caravan. He came from the district of Neggde, sent by a friendly sheik to warn the Drayhy of the rage into which his projects and alliances had thrown Ebn Sihoud. He despaired of seeing him ever able to make head against the storm, and strongly recommended him to make peace with the Wahabees. I wrote, in the name of the Drayhy, that he felt no more concern about Ebn-Sihoud than he should about a grain of mustard; placing his confidence in God, the sole giver of victory. Then, by a diplomatic *ruse*,

I gave him to understand that the armies of the Grand Signior would support the Drayhy, who was desirous, above all things, of opening the road to the caravans and delivering Mecca from the power of the Wahabees. The next day we crossed the great arm of the river in boats, and encamped at the other side, in the vicinity of the tribe of El Cherarah, celebrated for its courage, and also for its ignorance and obstinacy.

We had foreseen the extreme difficulty of gaining it over, not only on account of these faults, but because of the friendship which existed between its chief Abedd, and Abdallah, the principal minister of King Ebn Sihoud. Accordingly he refused to join the alliance; and in this state of things, the Drayhy, supposing all negotiation useless, declared that the sabre must decide between them. The following day Sahen was sent, with five hundred cavalry, to attack Abedd. He returned in three days, having taken one hundred and forty camels, and two mares of great value: eight men only were killed, but a great number wounded on both sides. I witnessed on this occasion a very extraordinary cure. A young man, a relation of Sahen, was brought back, having his skull broken by a stroke of the djerid, seven sabre wounds in the body, and a lance still fixed in his side. The extraction of the lance was immediately set about, and it was brought out from the opposite side: during the operation the patient turned to me and said —"Do not distress yourself about me, Abdallah, I shall not die;" and extending his hand, he took my pipe and began smoking as tranquilly as if the seven gaping wounds had been in another body.

In about twenty days he was completely cured, and was on horseback as before. The only medicine they gave him was camel's milk mixed with fresh butter, and his only food was dates dressed in butter. Every third day his wounds were washed in camel's urine. I doubt if a European surgeon, with all his apparatus, would have made so complete a cure in so short a time.

The war became daily more serious: Abedd collected his allies to surround us, which obliged us to encamp upon the sands of Caffera, where there is no water. The women were obliged to fetch it daily from the river, in leathern budgets carried by camels. The great quantity necessary for watering the cattle rendered this a very heavy labour. On the third day the terrified drivers came to announce that eight hundred camels had been carried off by Abedd's followers, while they were leading them to the river. The Drayhy, to revenge this outrage, gave orders to strike the tents and to make a rapid advance on the tribe of Cherarah, which he resolved to attack with his whole force. We marched a day and night without halting, and pitched ten thousand tents at about half a league from the camp of Abedd. A general and murderous battle seemed inevitable; but I determined to hazard a last effort to prevent it if possible.

The Bedouins hold women in great respect, and consult them on all their plans. In the tribe of El Cherarah their influence is even more extensive than elsewhere; there the women hold the actual command. They have generally much more sense than their husbands; and Arquia, wife of the Sheik Abedd, in particular passes for a very superior woman. I determined to go to her, to take her some presents of ear-rings, bracelets, necklaces, and other trifles, and to endeavour thereby to bribe her to our interests. Having secretly made all the necessary inquiries to direct my proceedings, I introduced myself to her in the absence of her husband, who was holding a council of war with one of his allies. By dint of compliments and presents, I led her to enter herself on the subject of the war,—the real purpose of my visit, though I did not choose to confess it. I took the opportunity of explaining to her the advantages of an alliance with the Drayhy, solely as a subject of conversation, and by no means as authorised to consult with her upon it: I told her that my visit was solely induced by a natural curiosity to see so celebrated a woman, who governed warriors redoubtable for their courage, but in need of her superior understanding rightly to direct their brutal force. During this conversation her husband returned to the camp, was informed of my arrival, and sent orders to Arquia ignominiously to dismiss the spy she had with her; that as the rites of hospitality would withhold his arm from taking vengeance upon the threshold of his own tent, he should not enter it till the traitor was gone. Arquia haughtily replied, that I was her guest, and that she should not suffer the law to be laid down to her. I got up to take leave of her, asking pardon for the embarrassment I had caused; but she seemed to make a point of convincing me that I had not gratuitously attributed to her an influence which she did not possess, for she detained me by force while she went to confer with her husband. She soon returned, accompanied by Abedd, who treated me very politely, and requested me to explain the intentions of the Drayhy. I gained his entire confidence, by the assistance of his wife, and, before the end of the day, he himself solicited permission to accompany me to the Drayhy; which I opposed, telling him that I should not dare to present him to the emir without notice, because he was so highly irritated against him; but that I would plead his cause and send him an immediate answer. I left them at least as desirous of joining the confederacy as I had been to persuade them to do so.

By the invitation of the Drayhy, Abedd went a few days afterwards to set his seal to the treaty, and to exchange the camels which had been reciprocally taken during the war. This difficult affair thus terminated in so satisfactory a manner, we left the sands to pass eight days in the district of Atteria, at three hours' distance from the Tigris, near the ruins of the castle El Attera, where the pasturage is abundant. Having here refreshed the cattle, we continued our route eastwards.

We one day met a Bedouin, mounted on a fine black dromedary: the sheiks saluted him with an air of concern, and inquired what had been the issue of his unfortunate adventure of the preceding year. I asked his history, and found the recital sufficiently interesting to give it a place in my journal. Aloian (this was the name of the Bedouin,) while hunting the gazelle, arrived at a spot were broken lances, bloody sabres, and unburied corpses indicated a recent battle. A plaintive sound, which scarcely reached his ear, attracted him to a pile of dead bodies, in the midst of which a young Arab still breathed. Aloian hastened to his assistance, placed him upon his dromedary, led him to his tent, and by his paternal cares restored him to life. After four months' convalescence, Faress (the wounded man) began to talk of his departure; but Aloian said to him:—"If we must absolutely separate, I will conduct you to your tribe, and there take leave of you with regret; but if you will remain with me, you shall be my brother, my mother shall be your mother, and my wife your sister: consider my proposal, and give it a deliberate answer."—"Oh! my benefactor," replied Faress, "where shall I find such relations as you offer me? But for you, I should not now be living; my flesh would have been devoured by birds of prey, and my bones by the beasts of the desert: since you are willing to keep me, I will live with you and serve you to the end of my life." A motive less pure than he dared to avow had prompted Faress's decision: love for Hafza, the wife of Aloian, who had been his nurse, was beginning to agitate his bosom, and was returned. Aloian, who entertained no suspicion, one day charged Faress to escort his mother, his wife, and two children to a new encampment, while he went hunting. Faress could not resist this fatal opportunity: he laded a camel with the tent, placed the mother and two children upon it, and sent them forward, saying that he would follow with Hafza on horseback. But the old woman looked back in vain: Hafza did not appear; Faress had carried her away upon an extremely swift mare to his tribe. In the evening Aloian arrived, fatigued with the chase, and searched in vain for his tent among those of his tribe. The old mother had been unable to pitch it without assistance, and he found her seated upon the earth with the two children. "Where is Hafza?" said he.—"I have neither seen Hafza nor Faress," replied she: "I have been expecting them since the morning." Then, for the first time, he suspected the truth; and having assisted his mother to fix the tent, he mounted his black dromedary and rode two days till he came up to the tribe of Faress. At the entrance of the camp he stopped to speak to an old woman who was alone. "Why do you not go to the sheik?" said she; "there is a feast in the tribe to-day: Faress Ebn Mehidi, who had been wounded on a field of battle and wept for dead, is returned, bringing with him a beautiful woman; this evening their wedding is to be celebrated." Aloian dissembled, and waited for the night: then, while all the camp slept, he introduced himself into the tent of Faress, separated his head from his body by a stroke of his sabre, and having carried the corpse out of the encampment, returned upon his steps, found his wife asleep, and woke her, saying,—"It is Aloian who calls thee; follow me." She rose in terror and said,—"Save thyself, imprudent man! Faress and his brothers will kill thee."—"Traitress!" replied he, "what have I done to be thus treated? Have I ever contradicted or reproached thee? Hast thou forgotten all the cares I have lavished upon thee? Hast thou forgotten thy children? Come, rise, call upon God and follow me: accursed be the devil who has tempted you to commit this folly!" But Hafza, far from being moved by this mildness of Aloian, exclaimed, "Go hence! or I shall give the alarm and call Faress to kill thee." Seeing that there was nothing to be gained by remonstrance, he seized her, stopped her mouth, and in spite of her resistance placed her on a dromedary, which never paused till they were out of hearing of the camp. Then placing her *en croupe* behind him, he more leisurely continued his route. At day-break the corpse of Faress and the disappearance of his wife set the whole camp in a tumult. His father and brothers followed and overtook Aloian, who defended himself with heroic courage. Hafza, breaking off her bonds, joined the assailants and threw stones at him, one of which struck him on the head and made him stagger. Aloian, however, though covered with wounds, conquered his adversaries: he killed the two brothers, and disarmed the father, saying it would be disgraceful to him to kill an old man; he restored him his mare, and advised him to return home; then, seizing his wife anew, he pursued his route and reached his tribe without having exchanged a word with her. He immediately assembled all her relations, and placing Hafza in the midst of them, said to her, —"Relate, thyself, all that has passed: I refer my cause to the judgment of thy father and brother." Hafza told the tale truly, and her father, full of indignation, raised his sabre and laid her at his feet.

Having proceeded stage by stage to within four hours of Bagdad, M. Lascaris secretly repaired thither to see the French consul, M. Adrien de Correncé, and negotiate with him for a large sum of money.

The next day, after crossing the Tigris at Machad, we established ourselves near the river El Cahaun, and learned there that a sanguinary war was raging between the Bedouins, who took part for or against our alliance. Sheik Ibrahim persuaded the Drayhy not to lose time, but to form a junction with our allies as expeditiously as possible. We consequently advanced, and encamped near many little springs, at twenty hours' distance from Bagdad; and the next day crossed a great chain of mountains: we then took the necessary precaution of filling our water budgets, having a march of twelve hours to make over burning sands, where neither water nor herbage is to be found. On reaching the frontiers of Persia we met a messenger of the tribe of El Achgaha, bearing a letter from the chief Dehass, who demanded the assistance of *the Father of Heroes—the chief of the most redoubtable warriors—the powerful Drayhy*, against enemies who number fifteen thousand tents. We were then at six days' journey from this tribe; but the

Drayhy having given orders to quicken the march, we accomplished this distance in three times twenty-four hours, without halting even to eat. The greatest fatigue of this forced march fell upon the women, who were obliged to make the bread and milk the camels, without delaying the caravan.

The organization of this ambulatory kitchen was very curious. At certain regulated distances women were placed, who were employed without relaxation. The first, mounted on a camel laden with wheat, had a handmill before her. The corn once ground, she passed the meal to her neighbour, whose business it was to knead it with water, carried in budgets suspended on the sides of her camel. The dough was then handed to a third woman, who baked it in the form of cakes on a chafing-dish, with charcoal and straw. These cakes she distributed to the division of warriors, whose food she was charged to provide, and who came every minute to demand their portion.

Other women walked beside the camels to milk them into *cahahs,*—wooden pails, containing four litres: these were passed from hand to hand to slake the thirst of the troops. The camels ate as they marched, from bags hung round their necks; and when their riders wished to sleep, they lay at their length on the camels, their feet secured in the sacks to protect them from falling. The slow and measured step of the camels invites to sleep, and I have never slept better than on this march. The wife of the Emir Faress was delivered in her howdah of a son, who received the name of Harma, from the place we were passing when he came into the world: it is at the confluence of the Tigris and Euphrates. We were soon after joined by three tribes: El Harba, El Suallema, and El Abdalla. We reckoned seven thousand tents when Dehass joined us. This imposing succour reassured him; we gave him a magnificent supper, after which he affixed his seal to our treaty.

The enemy was still at the distance of a day's journey. Our men and horses being in great need of repose, the Drayhy commanded a two days' rest; but the assailants did not allow us the desired truce. As soon as the report of our approach reached them, they began their march, and the next day thirty thousand men were encamped an hour from us. The Drayhy immediately advanced his army to the banks of the river, fearing that our supply of water might be intercepted; and we took up a position near the village of El Hutta.

The next day, the Drayhy sent a letter to the chiefs of the five tribes who were come to attack us: Douockhry, chief of El Fedhay; Saker Ebn Hamed, chief of El Modianu; Mohdi Ebn Hud, of El Sabha; Bargiass, of Mouayega; and Amer Ebn Noggies, chief of Mehayeda. This attempt was wholly unsuccessful: the answer was a declaration of war, the style of which clearly proved that our intentions had been misrepresented, and that the chiefs acted under foreign influence.

Sheik Ibrahim proposed to send me to them with presents, to endeavour to come to an explanation. My embassies had hitherto succeeded so well, that I accepted this with pleasure, and set out with a single guide: but scarcely had we reached the tent of Mohdi, who lay nearest to us, when their advanced guard came upon us like wild beasts, robbed us of our presents and our clothes, put irons on our feet, and left us naked on the burning sands. In vain I entreated permission to explain; I was threatened with instant death if I persisted in remonstrating. Some moments afterwards, I saw the perfidious Absi advancing to me: I then understood the cause of the inconceivable treatment of which I had been the victim; he had been travelling from tribe to tribe to raise enemies against us. I was so enraged at the sight of him, that my fallen courage revived, and I determined to die bravely if I could not live to take vengeance. He approached, and, spitting in my face, cried, " Dog of an infidel! in what manner do you choose that I should separate your soul from your body?"— " My soul," I replied, "is not in your power; my days are numbered by the great God: if they are to end now, it signifies little in what manner; but if I am still to live, you have no power to kill me." He then withdrew to excite the Bedouins against me afresh, and men, women, and children came to overwhelm me with outrages: some spit in my face, others threw sand in my eyes; several pricked me with their djerids. I was kept twenty-four hours without eating or drinking, and suffering a martyrdom it is impossible to describe. Towards the evening of the second day, a young man, named Jabour, came to me, and drove away the children who were tormenting me. I had already remarked him; for, of all those I had seen during this day, he alone had not insulted me. He offered to bring me bread and water at nightfall. "Hunger and thirst," I replied, thanking him, "are of little consequence; but if you could assist me to escape hence, I would reward you generously." He promised to attempt it, and in the middle of the night brought me the key of my fetters, which he had had the address to procure while the chiefs were at supper. He opened them without noise; and without taking time to throw on my clothes, we ran back to my tribe. All were asleep in the camp, except the four negroes who kept guard at the entrance of Drayhy's tent: they uttered a cry on seeing me, and in great haste woke their master, who came with Sheik Ibrahim: they embraced me with tears, and handsomely rewarded my liberator. The Drayhy expressed the most lively grief at the treatment I had experienced, and the greatest indignation at this violation of the rights of nations. He immediately gave orders for battle, and at sunrise we perceived that the enemy had done the same. On the first day, there was no marked advantage on either side. Auad, chief of the tribe Suallema, lost his mare, for which he had refused twenty-five thousand piastres. All the Bedouins participated in his affliction, and the Drayhy gave him one of his best horses, very inferior however to the superb animal he had lost. The next day the battle was renewed with increased fury, and our loss was more considerable than that of the enemy. We were obliged to act with extreme caution, having only fifteen thousand troops to oppose to him. Forty of our men fell into their hands, while we made only fifteen prisoners; but amongst these was Hamed, son of the chief Saker. The captives on both sides were put in irons.

To these two days of fighting succeeded a tacit truce of three, during which the two armies continued to face each other without any demonstration of hostility. On the third day, the chief Saker, with a single attendant, came to our camp. He was uneasy for his son, a valiant young man, adored by his father and by all the Bedouins of his tribe; and he came to ransom him. Hamed had been very well treated by us; I had myself bound up his wounds. The Drayhy received Saker with great distinction. The latter, after the customary civilities, spoke of the war—expressed his astonishment at the Drayhy's ardour against the Wahabees, and said that he could not credit so much disinterestedness, under which some secret motives or personal views must needs be couched. "You cannot take it ill," added he, "that I do not engage with you without knowing your object. Take me into your confidence, and I will second you to the utmost of my power." We replied, that we were not in the habit of admitting to our secrets those of whose friendship we had no assurance; but that if he chose to sign our treaty, we should have no concealments from him. He then asked to be made acquainted with this engagement, and after having listened to a lecture of the different articles, with which he seemed to be very well content, he assured us that things had been very differently represented to him, and repeated the calumnies that Absi had spread concerning us. He ended by affixing his seal to the treaty, and afterwards pressed us to explain the object we were aiming at. Sheik Ibrahim told him that our intention was to open a passage from the coasts of Syria to the frontiers of India, to an army of a hundred thousand men, under a powerful conqueror, who would relieve the Bedouins from the yoke of the Turks, restore to them the sovereignty of the country, and enable them to obtain possession of the treasures of India. He affirmed that there was nothing to be lost, but every thing to gain, in the execution of this project, the success of which depended upon the union of forces and the harmony of inclinations. He promised that their camels should be paid at a high price for the transport of the provisions for this great army, and made him look to the commerce of these vast countries as likely to become a source of inexhaustible riches to them.

Saker entered fully into our views; but it was still necessary to explain to him that the Wahabee[*] might counteract our plans; that his religious fanaticism would naturally be opposed to the passage of a Christian army; that his spirit of domination, which had already made him master of Yemen, Mecca and Medina, would extend his pretentions to Syria, where the

[*] Ebn Sihoud, King of the Wahabees, is often called by this name.

Turks could not offer him any serious resistance: that, on the other hand, a great maritime power, enemy to the one we favoured, would infallibly make an alliance with him, and would send forces by sea to cut us off from the road of the desert. After much debate, in which Saker showed both judgment and sagacity, he entirely acquiesced in our arguments, and promised to use all his influence with the other tribes. It was agreed that he should be chief of the Bedouins of the country we were then in, as the Drayhy was of those of Syria and Mesopotamia: he engaged between this time and the same period in the next year to unite the different tribes under his orders, while we should pursue our route; and promised that at our return all should be made easy to us. We separated, enchanted with each other, after loading his son with presents, and liberating all the other prisoners. Saker, on his part, sent back our forty men; and the next day wrote us word that Mohdi and Douackhry no longer opposed our projects, and that they were about to remove to hold a conference with Bargiass, at three hours' distance. In fact, they broke up their camp, and we did the same; for the assemblage of so large a number of men and cattle had covered the earth with filth, and rendered our continuance in the place quite intolerable.

We encamped at six hours' distance, at Maytal el Ebbed, where we rested eight days. Saker came there to us, and it was agreed that he alone should undertake to raise the Bedouins of these districts, while we should return into Syria, lest by too long abandoning our first conquest, our enemies should take advantage of our absence to embroil our affairs and detach the tribes from our alliance.

Besides, the spring was already advanced, and it behooved us to hasten thither, lest the pasturages of Syria and Mesopotamia should be occupied by others. We deferred then, till the year following, the project of pushing our recognizance as far as the frontiers of India. By that period, Saker would have had time to prepare the tribes of his neighbourhood to second us; "for," said he, "the tree is uprooted by one of its branches."

Some days' march brought us back to Mesopotamia. In two more we crossed the Euphrates near Mansour and the desert called El Hamad. We encamped in a place where water is only to be had by digging deep holes, and is at last only fit for the beasts. Man cannot drink of it. The place is called Halib El Dow, because milk is here the only beverage.

We went from thence to El Sarha, a district abundantly supplied with water and herbage, and here expected to be indemnified for our privations; but a particular circumstance speedily dashed our hopes. The soil is covered with an herb called *Kraffour*, which the camels eat with avidity, and which has the property of inebriating them to the point of madness. They run to the right and left, breaking every thing they encounter, overthrowing the tents, and pursuing the men.

During four-and-twenty hours no one could get any rest; the Bedouins were constantly employed in mastering the camels and in calming their fury. I should have preferred actual war to this continual struggle with animals whose prodigious strength, and delirious exaltation presented incalculable dangers. But it appears that the triumphs of skill over force has great charms for these children of nature; for, when I went to the Drayhy to deplore the state of fever in which this novel revolution held us, he only laughed, and assured me it was one of the greatest amusements of the Bedouins. While we were talking, a camel of the largest size made straight towards us, with his head erect, and kicking up the dust with his great feet. The Drayhy, seizing one of the stakes of his tent, waited for the furious animal, and struck him a violent blow on the head. The weapon broke, and the camel turned away to exercise his ravages elsewhere. A dispute then arose as to which was the strongest, the camel or the sheik. The latter averred, that if his club had resisted, he should have cleft the skull of his adversary; the attendants maintained the superiority of the animal, who had broken the obstacle opposed to him; and my decision, that their strength was equal, because it was a drawn battle, excited the mirth of the whole audience.

The next day we broke up our camp, and were overtaken on the road by a messenger from Saker, who sent us an account of the ill-success of his negotiation with Bargiass. Our enemy Absi, who was high in favour with the latter chief, had exasperated him against us; had persuaded him to join Mehanna, and then to form an alliance with the Wahabees, who were to send an army for our destruction. The Drayhy answered, that this was no cause for uneasiness—that God was stronger than they were, and could with ease give the victory to the good cause. After this incident we continued our journey.

We next learned that the tribe El Calfa was encamped at Zualma. The Drayhy considered it important to secure the co-operation of this powerful and courageous tribe. Its sheik, Giassem, was an old friend of the Drayhy; but he could neither read nor write, and it therefore became dangerous to address a letter to him, which would be read by a Turk, and might be essentially injurious to our affairs, as experience had taught us in the instance of the scribe Absi. Again, then, the negotiation was committed to me; and I was sent to him, with an escort of six men mounted on dromedaries. We arrived, after a journey of three days, at the spot indicated, and were greatly disconcerted to find that the tribe had removed their camp, leaving no trace of the road they had taken. We passed the night without eating or drinking, and deliberated the following day on what we were to do. The affair of most immediate necessity was to find water; for it is well known that thirst is more insupportable than hunger, and we might also reasonably expect at the same time to meet both with the springs and the tribe. We wandered three entire days without finding either water or food. My palate was so perfectly dry, that I could neither move my tongue nor articulate a sound; I had exhausted all the artificial means of mitigating thirst, as keeping pebbles and balls of lead in my mouth; my face was become black, and my strength was forsaking me, when suddenly my companions cried out, "Gioub el Ghamin!" (the name of a well in the desert,) and darted forward. These men, inured to fatigue, sustained privations in a manner inconceivable to me, and were far from imagining to what a deplorable condition I was reduced. On seeing them run from me, the irritation of my nerves, excited by fatigue, made me despair of reaching the well, where I fancied they would not leave a single drop of water for me; and I threw myself on the ground weeping. Seeing me thus overcome, they returned, and encouraged me to make an effort to follow them. We arrived at length at the well, and one of them leaning over the parapet, drew his sabre, declaring he would cut off the head of the first man who dared approach. "Be governed by my experience," said he, "or you will all perish." The authoritative tone he assumed had its effect upon us, and we all obeyed in silence. He called us one by one, beginning with me, and made us first lean over the margin of the well to inhale some of its moisture. Then drawing a small quantity of water, he wetted our lips with his fingers; by degrees he allowed us to drink a few drops, then a small cup full; and having pursued this rational treatment for three hours, he said, "You may now drink without risk; but if you had not listened to me, you would have been all dead men; for drinking without precaution, after long privation, is certain destruction." We passed the night on this spot, drinking continually, as much for nourishment as to slake our thirst, which, notwithstanding this indulgence, seemed insatiable. In the morning we climbed an eminence that we might see farther round us; alas! nothing but the boundless desert met our view. At length, however, one of the Bedouins thought he descried an object in the distance, and soon asserted that it was an howdah covered with scarlet cloth, and borne by a camel of great size. His companions saw nothing, but having no better guide to follow, we turned our steps in the direction indicated; and, in fact, soon afterwards we found ourselves approaching a great tribe, and distinctly saw the howdah which had served us for a pharos: happily it proved to be the tribe we were in quest of.

Giassem received us kindly, and did his best to remedy our fatigue. I satisfactorily accomplished the object of my mission to him, and he dictated a letter to the Drayhy, in which he undertook to place his men and goods under his orders, saying that the alliance between them ought to be of the closest kind, on account of their long-standing friendship. I set out on my return, provided with this important document, but, on the other hand, much interested in the news he had imparted to me of the arrival of a princess, daughter of the King of England, in

Syria, where she was displaying the luxuries of royalty, and had been received with all sorts of honours by the Turks. She had made magnificent presents to Mehanna el Fadel, and had been escorted by him to Palmyra, where she had profusely distributed her largesses, and had made a formidable party among the Bedouins, who had proclaimed her queen.* Sheik Ibrahim, to whom I carried this intelligence, was greatly disturbed by it, believing it to be an intrigue to ruin our plans.

The Drayhy, perceiving our misgivings, reassured us by declaring that if they sowed sacks of gold from Hama to the gates of India, they would be unable to detach a single tribe from the solemn engagement which had been contracted.

"The word of a Bedouin is sacred," he added; "follow up your projects without uneasiness. For my part, my campaign is planned. I am going to the Horan to watch the proceedings of Ebn Sihoud, whom alone we have cause to fear. I shall then return, and encamp in the environs of Homs."

Sheik Ibrahim, having no longer either money or merchandise, determined to send me immediately to Corietain, whence I should despatch a messenger to Aleppo to procure a supply of cash. I went joyfully, as the expedition gave me a prospect of visiting my friends and reposing some time amongst them. My first day's journey was performed without accident; but on the

* This imaginary princess was no other than lady Hester Stanhope.

following day, about four o'clock, at a spot named Cankoum, I fell into the midst of what I believed to be a friendly tribe, but which proved to be that of Bargiass. It was now too late to recede; I therefore made for the tent of the sheik, preceded by my negro Fodda: but scarcely had I set foot on the ground, when he was massacred before my eyes, and I saw the same weapons which had despatched him raised upon me. The shock was so great, that I have no recollection of what followed, except that I cried out, "Stop! I claim the protection of the daughter of Hedal!" and fainted. When I reopened my eyes, I found myself lying on a couch in a tent, surrounded by a score of females, who were endeavouring to recall me to life: some were holding burnt hair, vinegar, and onions to my nostrils; while others bathed me in water, and introduced melted butter between my dry and contracted lips. As soon as I had perfectly recovered my consciousness, the wife of Bargiass took me by the hand, saying:

"Fear nothing, Abdallah: you are in the tent of the daughter of Hedal, and no one has a right to injure you."

Bargiass presenting himself shortly afterwards at the entrance of the tent, to make his peace, as he said, with me,—"By the head of my father," cried she, "you shall not cross my threshold till Abdallah is entirely cured!"

I remained three days under Bargiass's tent, tended in the most affectionate manner by his wife, who was negotiating meanwhile a reconciliation between her husband and me; but I felt so rancorous a resentment at his brutality that I found it difficult to pardon him: at length, however, I consented to bury the past in oblivion, on condition of his signing the treaty with the Drayhy. We then embraced and entered into an oath of fraternity. Bargiass presented me with a negro, saying, "I have sacrificed your silver, but in return I give you a jewel;" a play of words upon the names of the two negroes, *Fodda*, silver, and *Gianhar*, jewel. He afterwards gave an entertainment in honour of our reconciliation. In the midst of the feast a courier arrived at full speed from the Drayhy, bringing to Bargiass a declaration of exterminating war, and full of the most opprobrious epithets. "Oh! thou traitor," he wrote, " who violatest the sacred law of the Bedouins! thou wretch for ever infamous, who massacrest thy guests! thou Ottoman under a black skin! know that all the blood of thy tribe would not suffice to compensate for that of my dear Abdallah! Prepare thyself for battle, for my courser will rest no more till I have destroyed the last of thy race!" I hastened my departure, to prevent any collision, and to comfort Sheik Ibrahim and the Drayhy. I cannot describe the joy and astonishment which my presence caused; and so miraculous did my return appear, that they could scarcely credit the evidence of their eyes, till I had related all my adventures.

The next morning I again took the road to Corietain, where I waited for twenty days the return of the messenger I had sent to Aleppo,—a respite which I found very seasonable both for repose and for the repair of my tattered wardrobe; but necessity protracted my stay beyond my inclination, for news was spread that the Wahabees had invaded the desert of Damascus and ravaged several villages, massacreing men and children without exception, and pillaging the women, whom alone they spared. The Sheik of Corietain, too weak to offer the smallest resistance, caused the gates of the town to be closed, forbade any egress from it, and tremblingly awaited the issue. We soon learned that the enemy having attacked Palmyra, the inhabitants had retired within the precincts of the temple, and there successfully defended themselves; and that the Wahabees, unable to force their position, had contented themselves with killing the camel-drivers and carrying off their camels. From thence they proceeded to ransack the village of Arack, and had dispersed themselves throughout the environs. This sinister intelligence alarmed me for the fate of my messenger, who however arrived safe and sound with Sheik Ibrahim's money. He had taken refuge for a short time at Saddad, the inhabitants of which having paid a pretty heavy contribution, had for the moment nothing more to fear. Profiting by this circumstance, I laid aside my Bedouin habiliments, and dressing myself as a Christian of Saddad, made my way to that village, where I obtained news of the Drayhy, who was encamped with the tribe of Bargiass at Ghandah el Cham. I rejoined him the first possible opportunity, and learned with chagrin that a formidable coalition had been effected between Mehanna el Fadel and the tribe established at Samarcand; and that by their intrigues with the governors of Hems and Hama, some Turks and Bedouins had been drawn into the alliance against us. In this critical conjuncture I bethought myself of our friend the Pacha Soliman, and persuaded Sheik Ibrahim to visit Damascus for the purpose of consulting with him. We set out at once, and alighted at the house of his prime minister, Hagim, from whom we learned the name of the supposed English princess: he informed us that it was through the influence of Lady Stanhope's presents that Mehanna had acquired so powerful a party amongst the Turks. These details confirmed our suspicions that England, aware of our projects, was subsidizing the Wahabees on one hand, while on the other she endeavoured, through the intervention of Lady Stanhope, to unite the Bedouins of Syria with the Turks. An Englishman, whom we met at the house of M. Chabassan, assuming the name of Sheik Ibrahim, added strength to these conjectures: he endeavoured to extract something from us, but we were too much upon our guard. Having obtained what we wished from Soliman Pacha, we hastened to rejoin our tribe.

The Drayhy's courage was not diminished; he assured us he could make head against a much stronger array. The firman granted us by Soliman Pacha required the governors of Hems and Hama to hold in respect his faithful friend and well-beloved son, the Drayhy Ebn Challan, who ought to be obeyed, being supreme chief of the Desert of Damascus; and that any alliance in opposition to him was contrary to the will of the

Porte. Furnished with this document, we advanced towards Hama; and some days afterwards Sheik Ibrahim received an invitation from Lady Hester Stanhope to pay her a visit in company with his wife, Madame Lascaris, who was still at Acre; an invitation that annoyed him the more, as he had for three years avoided sending any intelligence to his wife, in order to conceal from the world the place of his residence and his intimacy with the Bedouins. It was necessary, however, to send an answer to Lady Stanhope; he therefore wrote that he would do himself the honour of visiting her as early as circumstances would permit, and despatched at the same time a courier to his wife, desiring her to decline the invitation. But it was too late; Madame Lascaris, anxious to ascertain the existence of her husband, had instantly obeyed Lady Stanhope's summons to Hama, in hopes of gaining some traces of him from that lady: M. Lascaris thus found himself under the necessity of rejoining her.

Meanwhile Mehanna advanced nearer and nearer, fancying himself certain of co-operation from the Osmanlis; but the Drayhy, judging the time arrived for producing the pacha's firman, sent it to Hems and Hama by the hands of his son Saher, who was received with the greatest honours. After inspecting the order of which he was the bearer, the two governors placed their troops at his disposal, declaring Mehanna a traitor for calling in the Wahabees, the most inexorable enemies of the Turks.

Lady Hester Stanhope sent an invitation to

Saher, and overwhelmed him with presents for himself, his wife, and mother; gave a saddle and boots to every horseman of his suite, and announced her intention of shortly visiting his tribe. M. Lascaris' visit ended less agreeably: Lady Stanhope having vainly endeavoured, by questions ingeniously contrived, to draw from him some explanation of his connexion with the Bedouins, finally assumed a tone of authority which afforded M. Lascaris a pretext for a rupture. He sent his wife back to Acre, and quitted Lady Stanhope at open variance with her.

Mehanna made his dispositions for commencing the struggle; but finding the Drayhy by no means intimidated by his approach, he judged it prudent to secure a reinforcement of Osmanlis, and sent his son Fares to Hems, to claim the governor's promised assistance; who, however, instead of investing him with the command of a body of troops, had him loaded with irons and thrown into prison; and the dismayed Mehanna, at this afflicting intelligence, beheld himself precipitated in a moment from the supreme command, to the sad and humiliating necessity, not only of submission to the Drayhy, but of even soliciting his protection against the Turks. The unfortunate old man, overwhelmed by so unexpected a reverse, was obliged to implore the mediation of Assaf Sheik of Saddad, who promised him to negotiate a peace; and actually accompanied him with a hundred horsemen within a short distance of our camp. There leaving Mehanna with his escort, he advanced alone to the tent of the Drayhy, who received him very cordially, but refused at first to accept the submission of Mehanna, till we interposed in his behalf. Sheik Ibrahim represented the hospitality with which he had received us on our arrival in the desert, and Saher, twice kissing his father's hand, united his solicitations to ours. The Drayhy yielding at last, the principal men of the tribe marched forward to meet Mehanna, —an attention due to his years and rank. As soon as he alighted, the Drayhy assigned him the seat of honour in the corner of the tent, and ordered coffee to be brought. Mehanna hereupon rose: "I will drink none of thy coffee," said he, "till we shall be completely reconciled, and have buried the seven stones." At these words the Drayhy also rose; they drew and mutually presented their sabres to be kissed; after which they embraced, and the example was followed by their attendants. Mehanna with his lance made an opening in the ground, in the centre of the tent, about a foot in depth; and choosing seven small stones, he said to the Drayhy, "In the name of the God of peace, for your guarantee and mine, we thus for ever bury our discord." As the stones were cast into the hole, the two sheiks threw earth over them, and trod it down with their feet; the women signalizing the ceremony with deafening shouts of joy: at its termination the chiefs resumed their seats, and coffee was served.* From that moment it was no longer allowable to revert to the past, or to mention war. I was assured that a reconcilia-

---

* The ceremony is called the *hasnat*.

tion, to be according to rule, ought always to be solemnized in this form. After a plentiful repast, I read aloud the treaty, to which Mehanna and four other chiefs of tribes affixed their seals.*

Their united forces amounted to seven thousand six hundred tents; and, what was far more important still, the Drayhy became by this alliance chief of all the Bedouins of Syria, where he had no longer a single enemy. Saher went to Hems to solicit the deliverance of Fares, whom he brought back, attired in a pelisse of honour, to take part in the general rejoicing; after which the tribes dispersed, and occupied with their several stations the whole country from the Horan to Aleppo.

We now only waited the end of the summer to return towards the east, in order to conclude the negotiations we had commenced the preceding year with the tribes of Bagdad and Bussora; and this interval of calm and leisure was filled up with preparations for a marriage between Giarah, son of Fares, chief of the tribe El Harba, and Sabha, daughter of Bargiass, the most beautiful maiden of the desert. I was peculiarly interested in the affair, having known the bride during my residence with her mother. Fares begged the Drayhy to accompany him to Bargiass to make his proposals; and the chiefs of the tribe, in the richest attire, were in at-

* These chiefs were, Zarack Ebn Fahrer, chief of the tribe El Gioullan; Giarah Ebn Meghiel, chief of the tribe El Giahma; Ghaleb Ebn Ramdoun, chief of the tribe El Ballahiss; and Fares Ebn Nedged, chief of the tribe El Maslekher.

tendance. We reached the tent of Bargiass without any one being sent to meet us; Bargiass did not even rise to receive us: such is the usual form on such occasions; the smallest sign of forwardness would be considered unbecoming.

After a few moments' silence the Drayhy spoke;—"Why," said he, "do you receive us so indifferently? If you are resolved to offer us no refreshment, we will return home." During this time Sabha, withdrawn within that part of the tent reserved for the women, observed her suitor through the opening of the curtain; for custom exacts that the lady should signify her satisfaction at the appearance of her lover, before any negotiation is entered upon; and if, after the secret survey I have just mentioned, she gives her mother to understand that the intended bridegroom does not please her, the matter rests there. On this occasion, however, a young and handsome man, of a proud and noble presence, presented himself, and Sabha gave the requisite token of satisfaction to her mother, who then responded to the Drayhy's inquiry,—"You are all welcome! Not only will we heartily afford you refreshment, but we will grant all that you can desire."—"We come," returned the Drayhy, "to demand your daughter in marriage for the son of our friend: what do you require for her dowry?"—"A hundred nakas,"* replied Bargiass, "five horses of the race of Nedgde, five hundred sheep, three negroes, and three negresses to attend upon Sabha; and for the

* Female camels of the most beautiful species.

trousseau, a saddle embroidered with gold, a robe of damask silk, ten bracelets of amber and coral, and yellow boots." The Drayhy made some remonstrances on the exorbitance of the demand, saying, "Thou art minded to realize the Arab proverb: 'If thou wouldst not marry thy daughter, increase her price.' Be more reasonable if thou desirest the conclusion of this marriage."

The dowry was finally settled at fifty nakas, two horses, two hundred sheep, one negro, and one negress. The *trousseau* remained as dictated by Bargiass; saddles and yellow boots for the mother and some other members of the family were even added above his demand. Having written these articles, I read them aloud. Then the assistants at the ceremony recited the prayer *Faliha*—the Pater Noster of the Mussulmans, which confers its sanction on the contract,—and camel's milk was handed round, as lemonade had been at a town in Syria. After this refreshment the young people mounted their horses and amused themselves with the djerid,* and other games. Giarah, desirous to ingratiate himself with his bride, was particularly distinguished, and she remarked with pleasure his agility and grace. We separated at nightfall, and preparations for the nuptials now employed the thoughts of all.

By the evening of the third day, the dowry, or rather the price of Sabha, was ready, and a

* An equestrian exercise with sticks, called djerids, which are lanced like javelins.

numerous procession moved with it in the following order:—A horseman led the van, with a white flag pendent from the point of his lance, and crying, "I bear the spotless honour of Bargiass." After him followed the camels, decorated with garlands of flowers and foliage, attended by their drivers; then the negro on horseback, richly clothed, and surrounded by men on foot singing popular airs. Behind them marched a troop of warriors, armed with muskets, which they frequently discharged. A woman followed, sprinkling with incense a large vessel of fire which she carried. Then the milch ewes, under the guidance of their shepherds, who were singing like Chibouk, the brother of Antar, two thousand years earlier; for the manners of the Bedouins never change. After these came the negress, mounted upon a horse and evironed by two hundred women on foot, constituting not the least noisy of the groups; for the joyous shouts and nuptial songs of the Arab women are shrill beyond expression. The procession was closed by the camel which bore the *trousséau*, and formed a splendid spectacle. The embroidered housings were spread out on all sides and covered the animal; the yellow boots hung from his sides, and the jewels, arranged in festoons, completed his trappings. A child of one of the most distinguished families, mounted on this camel, repeated with a loud voice, "May we be ever victorious! May the fire of our enemies be extingushed for ever!" Other children accompanied him, crying, "Amen!" For my part, I ran from one side to the other, to enjoy the whole spectacle to the utmost.

This time Bargiass came out to meet us, attended by the horsemen and women of his tribe; the cries and chants then became truly deafening; and the horses galloping about on all sides, soon enveloped us in a whirlwind of dust.

When the presents were all displayed and ranged in order around the tent of Bargiass, coffee was made in a monstrous caldron, and every one took some, while waiting for the feast.

Ten camels, thirty sheep, and a prodigious quantity of rice formed the staple of the meal; after which a second caldron of coffee was emptied. The dowry accepted, the ceremony was concluded by a repetition of the prayer; and it was agreed that Giarah should come at the expiration of three days to fetch his bride. Before my departure, I visited the women in their apartments, to introduce Sheik Ibrahim to a more intimate acquaintance with Bargiass's wife, and to reiterate my thanks for her care of me. She replied by expressing her readiness to increase my obligations by bestowing her niece on me in marriage; but Sheik Ibrahim deferred taking advantage of her favourable intentions towards me till the following year.

On the eve of the day fixed for the wedding, a rumour arose that a formidable army of Wahabees had appeared in the desert: couriers flew from tribe to tribe, exhorting them to unite three or four in a company, that the enemy might find them prepared on all points to receive them; and the espousals had nearly been consummated by a mortal combat, instead of the sham fight which is customary on such occasions.

The Drayhy and the other chiefs set out very early in the morning with a thousand horsemen and five hundred women to achieve the conquest of the beautiful Sabha. At a short distance from the camp, the procession halted: the women and old men alighted and awaited the issue of a combat between the young people who came to carry off the betrothed, and those of her tribe who opposed their design. These contests have sometimes fatal results; but the bridegroom is not permitted to take part in them, lest his life should be exposed to hazard from the machinations of his rivals. On this occasion the combatants came off with about a score of wounds; and victory, as was reasonable, decided for our party, who carried off the bride in triumph and consigned her to the women of our tribe. Sabha's train was composed of a score of maidens with three well-laden camels; the first carrying her howdah covered with scarlet cloth, trimmed with fringes and tufts of various-coloured worsted, and adorned with ostrich-feathers: the interior was decorated by festoons of shells and strings of coloured glass, forming a sort of frames to small mirrors, which, placed at intervals, reflected the scene on all sides; and furnished with silken cushions for the reception of the bride. The tent formed the burden of the second camel, and the carpets and kitchen utensils that of the third. The queen of the festival being placed in her howdah, surrounded by the wives of the chiefs mounted on their camels, and by other women on foot, the procession commenced its retrograde march. Horsemen prancing in the van announced its progress to the tribes we might meet, who were expected to greet us by throwing incense and killing sheep under the feet of the bride's camels. It is not possible to convey a very exact idea of this scene, nor of that which lasted during the whole day and night; nor to describe the dances, the songs, the bonfires, the banquets, the tumult, and the cries of all sorts, which her arrival occasioned. Eight tribes were entertained by the hospitality of Fares. Two thousand pounds of rice, twenty camels, and fifty sheep, furnished out the feast; and in the middle of the night the cry was still, "Let him who is hungry come and eat." So great was my reputation among them, that Giarah begged a talisman from me to insure the happiness of this union: I accordingly wrote his cipher and that of his spouse in European characters; placed the charm solemnly in his hands; and no one doubted the efficacy of it, when they observed the satisfaction of the new-married couple.

Some days afterwards, hearing that the Wahabees, ten thousand strong, were besieging Palmyra, the Drayhy gave orders for marching against them. We encountered them at El Dauh, and exchanged some musket-shots till nightfall, but without coming to a pitched battle. I had here leisure to appreciate the advantage of the *mardouffs*, in these wars of the desert, in which it is always necessary to carry about the commissariat of the army, and often for a considerable time. These camels, mounted each by two soldiers, are like moving fortresses, provisioned with everything necessary for the nourishment and defence of their riders. A budget of water, a sack of flour and another of dried dates, a jar of sheep's butter, and the munitions of war, are formed into a sort of square tower on the animal's back. The men, conveniently placed on each side on seats composed of cordage, thus carry with them everything of which their temperate habits have need. When they are hungry, they knead a little of the meal with butter, and eat it in that state without baking; a few dates and a small quantity of water completing their moderate repast: nor do they quit their post to sleep, but throw themselves across the camel in the manner I have already described. The next day's engagement was more serious. Our Bedouins fought with more inveterate obstinacy than their adversaries, because their women and children were in their rear, while the Wahabees, far from home, and with no other object than pillage, were little disposed to risk their lives in the cause. Night separated the combatants, but with the earliest dawn the battle recommenced: at length, towards evening, victory declared in our favour; the enemy having lost sixty men killed, took to flight and left us in possession of the field of battle, besides twenty-two prisoners, forty beautiful mares, and sixty camels. This victory still enhanced the reputation of the Drayhy, and filled Sheik Ibrahim with joy; in the exuberance of which he exclaimed, "Thanks be to God, our affairs prosper!"

Having no longer any enemies to fear in the Syrian desert, Sheik Ibrahim parted company for a time from the Drayhy, and went to Hems to purchase merchandise and write to Europe. During our stay in that place he left me perfectly at liberty to seek amusement, and to recover from all my fatigues; and I made daily excursions into the country in company with some of my young friends, doubly enjoying this life of pleasure from its contrast with that which I had led amongst the Bedouins. But, alas! my joy was to be of short duration, and was soon converted into bitter anguish. A messenger, who had been to Aleppo to fetch remittances for M. Lascaris, brought me a letter from my mother, couched in terms of the deepest affliction, and announcing the death of my elder brother by the plague. Grief made her writing almost incoherent. She had been ignorant of my destiny for nearly the last three years, and conjured me, if still in existence, to go to her.

This dreadful intelligence deprived me of the use of my senses, and for three days I was unconscious where I was, and refused all nourishment. Thanks to the attentive care of M. Lascaris, I gradually recovered my recollection; but all that I could obtain from him was permission to write to my poor mother. Neither was I allowed to despatch my letter till the eve of our departure, for fear she should come herself to seek me. But I pass over the detail of my personal feelings, in which the reader can have no interest, to return to our travels.

The Drayhy having advertised us that he would shortly set out for the east, we hastened to join him, with three camels, two mares, and four guides, whom he had placed at our disposal. The day of our departure from Hems, I felt so extraordinary a weight upon my heart that I was tempted to regard it as a fatal presentiment. It struck me that I was advancing to a premature death. I made the best use, however, of my reasoning powers, and at length persuaded myself that the oppression I experienced resulted from the dejection into which my mother's afflicting letter had plunged me. We set out on a journey of twenty hours, and though wearied by travelling the whole day, were persuaded by our guides not to halt till we had completed it. Nothing particular occurred till midnight; when growing drowsy from fatigue and the monotonous movement of the march, we were alarmed by a sudden cry from the advanced guide—"Rouse yourselves, and look well about you, for we are on the brink of a tremendous precipice!" The road was but a foot in breadth; on the right was a perpendicular mountain, and on the left the precipice called Wadi el Hail. I woke in surprise, rubbed my eyes, and reseized the bridle, which I had allowed to hang loosely over the neck of my mare. But this precaution, which ought to have saved me, was the very thing that had nearly caused my death; for the animal having stumbled against a stone, fear made me draw the reins too hastily. She reared, and in coming down lost her footing, stepped only on vacancy, and rolled over with her rider to the bottom of the precipice. What passed after that moment of agony I know only from Sheik Ibrahim, who has since told me, that he dismounted in terror, and endeavoured to distinguish the nature of the gulf in which I had disappeared; but the night was too dark,—the noise of my fall was the only notice he had of it, and he could discern nothing but an abyss beneath his feet. He then betook himself to weeping, and conjuring the guides to go down the precipice. But this they declared impossible in the darkness, assuring him moreover, that it would be useless trouble, since I must not only be certainly dead, but dashed to pieces against the points of the rocks. Whereupon he announced his resolution not to stir from the spot till the daylight should enable him to make his researches, and promised a hundred tallarins to whoever should recover my body, however mutilated it might be, as he could not, he said, consent to leave it a prey to wild beasts. He then sat down on the edge of the gulf, waiting in mournful despair for the first glimmerings of daylight.

No sooner were they perceptible, than the four men descended the abyss with much difficulty, and found me, insensible, suspended by my sash, my head downwards. The mare lay dead a few toises below, at the extremity of the ravine. I had ten wounds on my head, the flesh torn from my left arm, my ribs broken, and my legs scratched to the bone. I was deposited, without any sign of life, at the feet of Sheik Ibrahim, who threw himself upon me in tears. But having a little knowledge of medicine, and carrying always some valuable remedies about with him, he did not long abandon himself to a useless grief. Having satisfied himself, by the application of volatiles to the nostrils, that I was not absolutely dead, he placed me carefully on a camel, and retraced his steps as far as the village of El Habedin. During this short journey my body swelled prodigiously, without giving any other sign of life. The village sheik having placed me on a mattress, sent to Hems for a surgeon. For nine whole hours I remained perfectly insensible; and at the end of that time opened my eyes without the smallest perception of the objects around me, or recollection of what had befallen me. I felt as if under the influence of a dream, but without being sensible of pain. In this state I lay for four-and-twenty hours, and recovered from my lethargy only to suffer such indescribable agonies that I fancied it would have been better a hundredfold to have remained at the bottom of the precipice.

Sheik Ibrahim never quitted me for an instant, and offered the highest rewards to the surgeon in case he should succeed in saving me. The latter was zealous, but by no means skilful; and no amendment appearing at the expiration of thirty days, gangrene was apprehended. The Drayhy had visited me immediately on being informed of my accident; and he also wept over me, and offered rich presents to stimulate the surgeon's efforts: but at the highest point of his sensibility he could not suppress his regret for the loss of his mare Abaige, who was of pure blood, and worth ten thousand piastres. Nevertheless, he was in real distress, as was Ibrahim; for they not only feared my loss, but foresaw in it the miscarriage of all their operations. I endeavoured to encourage them, telling them that I did not believe myself dying. But it was too true, that though, I should be spared, there was no probability of my being for a long while in a condition to travel.

The Drayhy was obliged to take leave of us to pursue his migration eastwards; and Sheik Ibrahim was in despair at seeing me grow daily worse. Hearing at length that a more skilful surgeon resided at El Dair Attia, he sent for him. The surgeon refused to come, requiring that the patient should be taken to him. I was therefore put upon a sort of litter in the best manner that could be contrived, and carried to him, at the hazard of expiring on the road. The new surgeon entirely changed the dressing of my wounds, and washed them with warm wine. Three months I stayed with him, suffering martyrdom, and a thousand times regretting the death I had escaped. I was then transported to the village of Nabek, where for three months longer I kept my bed. From that period I may date the actual commencement of my recovery, though it was retarded by frequent relapses. Upon the sight of a horse, for example, I fainted, and continued for a month in a state of extreme nervousness, which at length, and by degrees, I conquered: but I am bound to confess that to this moment the presence of that animal causes me a shudder;

and I made a resolution never again to mount a horse, except in a case of absolute necessity.

My illness cost Sheik Ibrahim five hundred tallarins. But how shall I estimate his attentions, his paternal care! I am assuredly indebted to him for my life.

During my convalescence he learnt that our friend the Pacha of Damascus had been replaced by another, Soliman Selim. This news greatly disconcerted us, as it appeared indicative of the loss of our credit with the Turks.

Ten months had elapsed—a second spring was come, and we were expecting with impatience the arrival of the Bedouins, our allies, when, to our great joy, a courier announced their approach. We forwarded him in haste to the Drayhy, who liberally rewarded him for the good news he brought of my recovery, which produced universal joy in the camp, where I had long been supposed dead. We waited some days longer, till the tribe advanced nearer; and in the interval a singular story came to my knowledge, which I think worthy of insertion, as an illustration of Arab manners.

A merchant of Anatolia, escorted by fifty men, was leading ten thousand sheep to be sold at Damascus. On the road he made acquaintance with three Arabs, with one of whom he formed a close intimacy, and at parting was desired to swear fraternity with him. The merchant could not discover in what respect he, who was the proprietor of ten thousand sheep, and was escorted by fifty soldiers, could be benefitted by having a brother amongst the poor

Bedouins; but the Bedouin, whose name was Chatti, was so importunate, that, to satisfy him, he consented to give him two piastres and a handful of tobacco as pledges of fraternity. Chatti divided the two piastres between his companions, saying, " Be ye witnesses that this man is become my brother." They then separated, and the merchant thought no more of the matter, till, at a place called Ain el Alak, a party of Bedouins, superior in number to his escort, attacked and routed them, took possession of his sheep, and stripped him to his shirt; in which pitiable condition he arrived at Damascus, imprecating curses upon the Bedouins, and especially upon his pretended brother Chatti, whom he accused of betraying and selling him.

Meanwhile the news of so rich a capture was quickly spread in the desert, and reached the ears of Chatti, who, having with some difficulty found his two witnesses, brought them before Soultan el Brrak, chief of the tribe of El Ammour, to whom he declared that he was brother to the merchant who had just been robbed, and called upon the chief to enable him to fulfil the duties of fraternity, by restoring the property. Soultan, having taken the depositions of the two witnesses, was obliged to accompany Chatti to El Nahimen, the sheik of the tribe which had carried off the sheep, and to reclaim them in conformity with their laws. The sheik was under the necessity of restoring them; and Chatti, having first ascertained that none were missing, took the road to Damascus, with the flocks and their shepherds.

Leaving them outside the town, he entered it in search of his brother, whom he found seated in a melancholy mood in front of a coffee-room of the Bazaar. He went straight to him with a joyful air; but the other turned angrily away, and Chatti had great difficulty in obtaining a hearing, and still greater in persuading him to believe that his sheep were waiting for him outside the walls. He apprehended a new snare, and would not for a long while consent to follow the Bedouin. Convinced at last by the sight of his sheep, he threw himself on Chatti's neck, and after giving full expression to his gratitude, vainly exerted himself to induce him to accept a recompense proportioned to such a service. The Bedouin could only be persuaded to receive a pair of boots and a *cafia* (handkercheif), not worth above a tallarin at the utmost, and, after partaking of his brother's bread, returned to his tribe.

Our first interview with the Drayhy was truly affecting. He came himself, with the principal members of his tribe, to seek us at the village of Nabek, and took us back in a sort of triumph to the camp. By the way he gave us the history of the wars he had waged in the territory of Samarcand, and his good fortune in vanquishing four of the principal tribes,* and afterwards inducing them to sign the treaty. It was important to have detached these tribes in

* The tribe El Krassa, whose chief was Zahaman Ebn Houad; the tribe El Mahlac, with its chief Ebn Habed; the tribe El Meraikhrat, its chief Roudan Ebn Abed; and the tribe El Zeker, its chief Matlac Ebn Fayhan.

time from their alliance with the Wahabees, to whom they were formerly tributary ; for it was reported that our enemies were preparing a formidable army, and flattered themselves with obtaining the supremacy of all Syria. Soon afterwards we heard that the army was on its march, spreading terror and devastation everywhere on its passage.

The Pacha of Damascus despatched orders to the governors of Hems and Hama, to keep guard day and night, and to hold their troops in readiness for battle: while the inhabitants fled towards the coast, to escape the sanguinary Wahabees, whose name alone sufficed to drive them from their homes.

The Drayhy was invited by the pacha to a conference with him at Damascus; but fearing some treason, he excused himself under pretence of the impossibility of deserting his post at so critical a moment. He even requested from him some auxiliary troops, hoping by their assistance to be able to keep the enemy in check.

While waiting for the expected reinforcement, the Drayhy caused a solemn declaration of war to be made, according to the custom of the Bedouins on very particular occasions, in the following form:—A white female camel was selected, and blackened all over with soot and oil; reins made of black hair were then put over her, and she was mounted by a young maiden dressed in black, with her face and hands also blackened. Ten men led her from tribe to tribe, and on reaching each she proclaimed aloud three times,—" Succour! succour! succour! Which of you will make this camel white? she is a relic from the tent of the Drayhy menacing ruin. Fly, fly, noble and generous defenders! The Wahabees are coming! they will carry away your allies and your brothers: all you who hear me, address your prayers to the prophets Mahomet and Ali, the first and the last!"

Saying which, she distributed amongst the tribe handfuls of black hair, and letters from the Drayhy, indicating the place of rendezvous on the banks of the Orontes. Our camp was in a short time augmented by the coalition of thirty tribes, assembled in the same plain, and so thickly encamped that the ropes of our tents touched. The Pacha of Damascus sent ten thousand men to Hama, commanded by his nephew Ibrahim Pacha, there to wait for other troops which the Pachas of Acre and Aleppo were to furnish. Scarcely had they met, when the arrival of the Wahabees at Palmyra was announced by the inhabitants, who fled to take refuge in Hama. Ibrahim Pacha wrote to the Drayhy, who repaired to him, and they arranged together their plan of defence. The Drayhy, who took me with him as his counsellor, acquainted me with the stipulations agreed upon; when I pointed out to him the danger of uniting Bedouins and Turks in the same camp, the latter having no means of distinguishing in the confusion of battle their friends from their enemies. The Bedouins themselves, indeed, recognize each other in the heat of the fight only by their war-cries, each tribe incessantly repeating its own,—"Khrail el allia Doualli,—Khrail el bionda Hassny,—Khrail el hamra Daffiry," &c.;—Khrail signifying horsemen; allia, bionda, hamra, indicating the colour of their favourite mare; Doualli, Hassny, Daffiry, are the names of the tribes. This war-cry, therefore, is equivalent to the words, *horsemen of the red mare of Daffir*, &c. Others invoke their sister, or some other beauty; hence the Drayhy's war-cry is, Ana Akhron Rabda,—I the brother of Rabda; that of Mehanna,—I the brother of Fodda: both have sisters renowned for their beauty. The Bedouins pride themselves greatly in their war-cries, and would consider that man a coward who should hesitate to pronounce it in the moment of danger. The Drayhy saw the force of my argument, and persuaded Ibrahim Pacha, though with difficulty, to consent to a division of their forces.

The next day we returned to the camp, followed by the Mussulman army, composed of Dalatis, Albanese, Mogrebins, Houaras, and Arabs; in all, fifteen thousand men. They had with them some pieces of ordnance, a few mortars and bombs, and pitched their tents half an hour's march from ours: the pride of their bearing, the variety and richness of their costumes, and their banners, altogether formed a magnificent spectacle; but, in spite of their fine appearance, the Bedouins jested upon them, and asserted that they would be the first to fly.

In the afternoon of the second day a broad cloud was observable towards the desert, spreading itself like a thick fog as far as the eye could reach: by degrees the cloud cleared up, and the enemy's army appeared in view.

This time they brought their wives, their children, and their camels, and established their camp, composed of fifty tribes, forming seventy-five thousand tents, at an hour's march from ours. About each tent, camels and a great number of sheep were tied ; presenting, together with the horses and warriors, a formidable mass to the eye. Ibrahim Pacha was in consternation, and sent in great haste in search of the Drayhy, who, having succeeded in reanimating his courage a little, returned to the camp, to order the necessary entrenchments. For this purpose all the camels were assembled, bound together by their knees, and placed in double files in front of the tents; and, to complete the rampart, a trench was dug behind them. The enemy on his part did the same, and the Drayhy ordered the Hatfé to be prepared. This singular ceremony consists in selecting the most beautiful amongst the Bedouin girls, to be placed in a houdah, richly ornamented, borne by a tall white camel. The choice of the maiden who is destined to occupy this honourable but perilous post is very important, for the success of the battle depends almost entirely upon her. Placed opposite to the enemy, and surrounded by the bravest warriors, it is her duty to excite them to the combat: the principal action always takes place around her, and prodigies of valour defend her. All would be lost should the hatfé fall into the enemy's hands; and, to avoid so irreparable a misfortune, half the army must always be stationed about her. Warriors succeed each other on this point, where the battle is always hottest, and each comes to gather enthusiasm from her looks. A girl named Arkia, uniting in an eminent degree courage, eloquence and beauty, was chosen for our hatfé. The enemy also prepared his, and the battle soon afterwards commenced. The Wahabees divided their army into two corps: the first and most considerable, commanded by Abdallah el Hedal, the general-in-chief, was opposed to us; the second, under the command of Abou Nocta, to the Turks. Both the character of the latter, and their mode of fighting, are totally different from those of the Bedouins, who, prudent and cool headed, begin the action calmly, but growing gradually animated, become at last furious and irresistible. The Turk, on the contrary, proud and arrogant, rushes impetuously upon the enemy, and fancies he has only to appear and conquer: his whole energy is thus expended on the first shock.

The Pacha Ibrahim, seeing the Wahabees attack coldly, deemed himself sufficiently strong to disperse their entire army without assistance; but, before the end of the day, he had learned by dear-bought experience to respect his enemy, and was forced to permit his troops to fall back, leaving us to sustain the whole weight of the action.

Sunset suspended the engagement, but not till both parties had suffered a severe loss.

The next morning brought us a reinforcement, in the tribe of El Hadidi, four thousand strong, all mounted on asses, and armed with muskets. We numbered our forces, which amounted to eighty thousand men; but the Wahabees had a hundred and fifty thousand, and this day's battle terminated in their favour. Our defeat, exaggerated, as always happens in similar cases, was reported at Hama, and filled the inhabitants with dismay; but two days afterwards their fears for us were removed, and for three weeks we were alternately discomfited and successful. The actions became daily more sanguinary; and on the fifteenth day of this trying campaign, a new enemy, more formidable than the Wahabees, arose in the shape of famine. The town of Hama, which alone could furnish subsistence to either army, was exhausted, or concealed its resources. The Turks took to flight; our allies dispersed, to avoid perishing with hunger; the camels, forming the rampart of our camp, began to devour one another. Amidst such frightful calamities, the courage of Arkia never for an instant wavered. The bravest of our warriors were slain by her side; but she ceased not to encourage them, and to excite and applaud their efforts. She animated the old by extolling their valour and experience; the young, by the promise of marrying him who should bring her the head of Abdallah el Hedal. Keeping my station near her houdah, I saw all the warriors present themselves to her for some words of encouragement, and then rush to the combat, excited to enthusiasm by her eloquence. I confess I preferred hearing these compliments to receiving them myself, for they were almost uniformly the forerunners of death.

I one day saw a fine young man, one of our bravest soldiers, present himself before the houdah: "Arkia," said he, "O thou fairest amongst the fair, allow me a sight of thy face, for I go to fight for thee!" Arkia, unveiling, replied: "Behold, O thou most valiant! Thou knowest my price; it is the head of Abdallah!" The young man brandished his spear, put spurs to his courser, and rushed into the midst of the enemy. In less than two hours he sank covered with wounds. "Heaven preserve you!" said I to Arkia, "this brave man is killed."—"He is not the only one who has never returned," she sorrowfully replied. At this moment a warrior made his appearance, armed from head to foot; even his boots were defended with steel, and his horse covered with a coat of mail, (the Wahabees reckoned twenty such warriors amongst them; we had twelve.) He advanced towards our camp, challenging the Drayhy to single combat: this has been the custom amongst the Bedouins from time immemorial; he who is thus defied, cannot without forfeiting his honour refuse to fight. The Drayhy, hearing his name, prepared to answer to the challenge: but his kinsmen joined with us to prevent it. His life was of too much importance to be thus risked; for the loss of it would have entailed the total ruin of our cause, and the destruction of the two allied armies. Persuasion becoming useless, we were obliged to have recourse to coercion. We bound him with cords hand and foot to stakes driven into the ground in the middle of his tent: the most influential chiefs supported him, and entreated him to calm himself, urging the imprudence of risking the welfare of the army for the purpose of answering the insolent bravado of a savage Wahabee. Meanwhile, the latter incessantly exclaimed : " Let the Drayhy come forth! this shall be his last day ; I am waiting to terminate his career." The Drayhy, who heard him, becoming more and more furious, foamed with rage and roared like a lion ; his blood-shot eyes almost starting from his head, while he fought with terrible strength to disencumber himself of his bonds. This tumult attracted a considerable multitude around the tent, when suddenly a Bedouin, making his way through the crowd, presented himself before the Drayhy. His sole clothing was a shirt bound round his loins with a leathern girdle, and a turban on his head; he was mounted upon a bay horse, and armed only with a spear; and thus singularly equipped, he came to ask, in the following metrical style, permission to fight the Wahabee instead of the sheik : " This day, I, Tehaisson, have become master of the horse Hadidi : it has long been the object of my ambition; I wished to receive upon his back the praises due to my valour. I am about to fight and to vanquish the Wahabee, for the beautiful eyes of my betrothed, and to render myself worthy of his daughter who was always conqueror." So saying, he rushed to combat the hostile warrior. No one imagined that he could for one half hour resist his formidable antagonist,

whose armour rendered him invulnerable; but if
the blows he dealt were thus robbed of their
murderous power, he avoided with wonderful
dexterity those that were aimed at himself during
the two hours that the struggle lasted. Meanwhile, all was suspense; the deepest interest was
manifested on both sides. At length our champion turned round, and apparently took to flight.
All hope was now lost; the enemy was about to
proclaim his triumph. The Wahabee pursued,
and, with a hand strengthened by the assurance
of success, flung his lance; but Tehaisson, foreseeing the blow, stooped even to his saddle-bow,
and the weapon flew whizzing above his head;
then, suddenly returning, he thrust his spear into the throat of his adversary, taking advantage
of the moment when the latter, being obliged to
curb his horse hastily before him, was in the act
of raising his head. This movement leaving a
space between the helmet and the cuirass, the
spear passed through from side to side, and killed
him on the spot: but his armour supporting him
in the saddle, he was carried by his horse into
the midst of his followers; and Tehaisson returned
in triumph to the tent of the Drayhy, where he
was enthusiastically rece ved. All the chiefs
embraced him, loading him with eulogies and
presents; and Sheik Ibrahim was not backward
in testifying his gratitude.

Meanwhile, the war and the famine continued
to rage: even in the Drayhy's tent we were two
days without food; on the third, he received a
considerable supply of rice, which Mola Ismael,
chief of the Dallatis, sent him as a present. Instead of husbanding it as a last resource, he or-

dered that the whole should be dressed, and invited all present to sup with him. His son Saher would not sit down to table; but, being importuned by his father, he requested that his portion might be given to him, and carried it to his mare, declaring that he had rather suffer himself, than see her die for want of food.

We had now arrived at the thirty-seventh day from the commencement of the war: on the thirty-eighth, the battle was terrible. The camp of the Osmanlis was taken and pillaged: the pacha had scarcely time to escape to Hama, whither he was pursued by the Wahabee, who there besieged him.

The defeat of the Turks was the more fatal to us, as it left the second corps of the hostile army, commanded by the famous Negro Abou Nocta, at liberty to unite with Abdallah, and make a combined attack upon us. The following day witnessed the commencement of a frightful struggle, which lasted eight days without intermission. The combatants were so intermingled together, that it was impossible to distinguish one party from another. They fought with the sabre man to man; the entire plain was deluged with blood, the colour of the ground being totally invisible: never perhaps was such a battle fought. The inhabitants of Hama, fully persuaded that we were utterly exterminated, no longer sent us those occasional supplies of provisions which, coming at our utmost need, had hitherto preserved us from starvation. At length the Drayhy, finding his misfortunes accumulate, assembled his chiefs, and addressed them thus: "My friends, it now becomes necessary that we should make a last effort. To-morrow we must either conquer or die. To-morrow, by God's permission, I will destroy the enemy's camp: to-morrow we will feast upon its spoils." This harangue was received with a smile of incredulity; until one, more daring than the rest, replied: "Give but the word, and we will obey."—"This night," he continued, "you must noisely transplant your tents, your wives, and your children, to the other side of the Orontes. The whole must have disappeared before sunrise, without the cognisance of the enemy. Then, having no longer any care to trouble us, we will make a desperate attack upon them, and will exterminate them, or perish ourselves in the attempt: but God will be on our side, and we shall conquer." Every one hastened to execute the commands thus given, with incredible order, celerity, and silence. The next day, the efficient warriors alone remained. The Drayhy divided them into four corps, ordering a simultaneous attack upon the four sides of the enemy's camp. The troops, in desperation, threw themselves upon their prey like hungry lions; and the impetuous but well-concerted onset was attended with all the success which could have been wished. Confusion and disorder spreading rapidly amongst their unexpectedly enclosed ranks, the Wahabees took to flight, abandoning their women and children, their tents and their baggage. The Drayhy, without allowing his men time to seize upon the booty, obliged them to pursue the fugitives to Palmyra, and gave them no respite until they had accomplished the total dispersion of the enemy.

No sooner had victory declared itself in our

favour, than I departed with Sheik Ibrahim to announce the joyful intelligence at Hama; but nobody there would give credit to it, and the inhabitants would fain have treated ourselves as fugitives. They exhibited the utmost perturbation: some climbed the heights, whence they could perceive nothing but clouds of dust; others prepared their mules for flight towards the coast. The defeat of the Wahabees being, however, speedily confirmed, the most extravagant demonstrations of joy succeeded to this terrible alarm. A Tartar was despatched to Damascus, and brought back with him forty loads of wheat, twenty-five thousand piastres, and a sabre and a robe of honour for the Drayhy, who made his triumphal entry into Hama, escorted by all the chiefs of the allied tribes. He was received by the governor, the agas, the pacha, and all his court, in the most splendid manner.

After four days of rejoicings we quitted Hama, to rejoin our tribes, and conduct them to the east before the approach of winter. The Drayhy was personally attended by a company of twelve; the others, in groups of five or six, dispersed themselves in the desert of Damascus. Our first stay was at Tall el Dehab, in the territory of Aleppo, where we encountered four tribes who had taken no part in the war. The chiefs came forward to meet the Drayhy, penetrated with respect for his recent exploits, and soliciting the favour of being admitted to sign the treaty of alliance with us.* From thence we

* Fares Ebn Aggib, chief of the tribe El Bechakez, with five hundred tents; Cassan Ebn Unkban, chief of the tribe El Chi-

marched without interruption to join our friend, the Emir Faher, who received us with the most lively demonstrations of joy. In company with his, and several other tribes, proceeding like ourselves to Mesopotamia, we crossed the Euphrates, some establishing themselves in the neighbourhood of Hamad, others in the desert of Bussora.

On the road we received a letter from Fares el Harba, announcing that six considerable tribes, who had fought on the side of the Wahabees against us, were encamped in the Hebassia, near Machadali, and were well disposed to enter into alliance with us; and that if the Drayhy would send me to him furnished with full powers to treat, he believed himself certain of success. I lost not a moment in availing myself of this invitation, and, after a journey of six hours, reached him without accident. Fares el Harba immediately broke up his camp, and conducted me to the distance of a day's journey from the tribes.* I then wrote in his name to the Emir Douackhry, chief of the tribe El Fedhan, exhorting him to make an alliance with the Drayhy, and promising oblivion of the past. Douackhry came in person to Fares el Harba, and we were soon agreed; but he disclaimed answering for more

---

amssi, one thousand tents; Selame Ebn Nahssan, chief of the tribe El Fuaher, six hundred tents; Mehanna el Saneh, chief of the tribe El Salba, eight hundred tents.

* The tribe of El Fedhan, composed of five thousand tents; that of El Sabha, four thousand tents; El Fekaka, one thousand five hundred; El Messahid, three thousand five hundred; El Salca, three thousand; finally, that of Benni Dehabb, five thousand.

than his own tribe, considering that it would be extremely difficult to succeed with the others. He proposed, however, that I should accompany him back, when he would assemble the chiefs of all the tribes, and exert his utmost influence with them. I accepted the invitation, and departed with him; but when arrived in the centre of what ought to have been an encampment, I was painfully affected to behold hordes of Arabs crouching on the ground under the full blaze of the sun: having lost their tents and baggage in the battle, their only bed was the bare ground, their only canopy the sky. A few rags suspended here and there upon pikes did indeed afford a semblance of shade to these unfortunate beings, who, having stripped themselves of their only garments to furnish this slender shelter from the fervent heat of the sun, were exposed to the sting of insects, and to the thorny points of the plants on which their camels browse. Many were wholly destitute of any defence either from the heat of day or the cold of night, at that autumnal season, when the contrasts of temperature are most fatal.

Never had I conceived an idea of wretchedness so complete: the sad spectacle oppressed my heart and drew tears from my eyes, and it was some time before I could recover from the agitation it occasioned me.

The next day Douackhry assembled the chiefs and old men to the number of five hundred. Alone in the midst of them, I despaired of making myself heard, and especially of being able to unite them in one counsel. Independent in their character and manners, and irritated by misfortune, they all mooted different opinions; and if neither hoped to make his own prevail, at least each made it a point of honour to maintain it obstinately, leaving all the others at liberty to do the like. Some proposed removing to the Nedgde country, others to retire to Samarcand: these vociferated imprecations against Abdallah, chief of the Wahabee army; those denounced the Drayhy as the author of all their misfortunes. Amid the conflict of voices, I armed myself with patience, and endeavoured to conciliate all parties. I began by shaking their confidence in the Wahabees; showing them that Abdallah must necessarily have become their enemy, since they had abandoned him on the last day of the battle, and that he was now seeking vengeance upon them: that in going to Nedgde they voluntarily threw themselves under the domination of Ebn Sihoud, who would extort from them oppressive contributions, and compel them to bear the whole burden of a disastrous war: that having once deserted his cause, and effected their withdrawal from his power, they should not follow the example of the foolish bird, who no sooner escapes the sportsman's shot than he falls into the fowler's net. At last, the fable of the bundle of sticks occurred to my mind; and thinking so simple a demonstration would make an impression on their unsophisticated minds, I determined to make a practical application of it before their eyes. Having exhorted them to be united, and by their union to resist all oppression, I took from the hands of the sheiks about thirty djerids, and presented one to the Emir Fares, requesting he would break it, which he effected with ease. I then presented him with two, and afterwards with three, all of which he broke in the same manner, for he was a man of great muscular strength. I then placed in his hand the whole bundle, which he could neither break nor bend. "Machala," said I, "thy strength is not sufficient;" and I then passed the united spears to another, who succeeded no better. A general murmur now arose in the assembly: "Who could split such a mass?" cried they unanimously. "I take you at your word," said I; and in the most energetic language I could command, I applied the apologue to their reasoning faculties,—adding, that so powerfully had I been affected by their destitute condition, without clothing or shelter, that I pledged myself to solicit from the Drayhy the restitution of their baggage and tents, and that I was sufficiently acquainted with his magnanimity to answer for the success of my application, if they entered heartily into the alliance, of which I had just proved the advantages. Upon this they all exclaimed with one voice: "Thou hast conquered, Abdallah; we are thine in life and in death!" and all ran forward to embrace me. It was then determined that they should give the Drayhy the rendezvous in the plain of Halla, to affix their seal to the treaty.

Recrossing the Euphrates the next morning, I rejoined our tribe on the fifth day, and found my friends uneasy at my protracted absence; but the report of my fortunate negotiation filled them with joy. I have already so frequently detailed meetings, feasts, and rejoicings of every kind, that I shall not repeat the same narrative by describing those which took place on this occasion.

The Emir Douackhry buried the seven stones, and thus consummated the alliance; and after dinner I witnessed for the first time the ceremony of swearing fidelity over bread and salt. The Drayhy then declared that he was ready to fulfil the engagement I had contracted in his name, by restoring the booty taken from the six tribes who had just united their cause with his. But the generous will was insufficient—the means of its execution were still to be provided. In the pillage of the Wahabee and allied camp, the plunder of fifty tribes was confounded, and to identify the property of each was no easy matter. It was decided that the women alone were competent to the task; and it would be impossible to form an idea of the exertion and fatigue of the five days employed by them in recognising the cattle, tents, and baggage of the various tribes. Every camel and sheep has two ciphers stamped with a hot iron on the leg, those of the tribe and the proprietor. But when, as it often happens, the ciphers are similar, or half effaced, the difficulty of identifying them is extreme; and under the exhausting task of reconciling such various pretensions, and deciding such harassing controversies, which it required something more than generosity to endure with patience, I was sometimes tempted to repent my momentary impulse of compassion and my imprudent promise.

At this time a great caravan from Bagdad to Aleppo passed, and was plundered by the Fedans and Sabhas. It was very richly laden with indigo, coffee, spices, Persian carpets, Cashmires, pearls, and other valuable articles, which we estimated at ten millions of piastres. No sooner was the capture known, than merchants flocked to the desert, some from a great distance, to purchase these treasures from the Arabs, who sold, bartered, or rather gave them away almost for nothing. For instance, they exchanged a measure of spices against an equal measure of dates; a Cashmire shawl, worth a thousand francs, against a black saddle-cloth; a chest of indigo for a linen dress; entire pieces of India muslin for a pair of boots. A merchant from Moussoul bought, for a shirt, a saddle-cloth, and a pair of boots, goods worth fifteen thousand piastres; and a diamond ring was sold for a roll of tobacco. I might have made my fortune on the occasion, but M. Lascaris prohibited my either purchasing or receiving any thing as a gift, and I scrupulously obeyed. Every day tribes arrived from the Nedgde country, deserting the Wahabees to join us; some attracted by the Drayhy's extraordinary reputation, others driven by dissensions with King Ebn Sihoud. One circumstance of that nature brought us five tribes in a body. The emir of the tribe Beny Tay had a very beautiful daughter, named Camara (the moon); Fehrab, son of the chief of a neighbouring tribe, and a relative of the Wahabee, became enamoured of her, and contrived to gain her affection; but the girl's father discovering their passion, forbade her speaking to the prince, and himself refused to receive him or listen to his proposals, designing Camara for her cousin

Tamer; for it is a custom amongst the Bedouins, which reminds one of those transmitted to us by the Bible, for the nearest kinsman to be preferred to all other suitors when a maiden's marriage is in question.

Camara, however, neither swayed by the usages of her people, nor intimidated by her father's menaces, positively refused to espouse her cousin; and her attachment acquiring strength in proportion to the obstacles opposed to it, she lost no opportunity of corresponding with her lover. The latter, seeing no hope of obtaining her parent's consent, resolved to run away with her, and opened the proposition to her through an old woman whom he had gained. She gave her consent; and he introduced himself into the tribe Beny Tay in the disguise of a mendicant, and arranged with her the hour and circumstances of the elopement. In the middle of the night the maiden stole fearfully out of her father's tent, to the prince, who was waiting for her at the entrance of the camp. He placed her behind him on his mare, and dashed across the plain; but the celerity of their flight could not conceal them from the jealous eye of Tamer: enamoured of his cousin, and determined to maintain his right, he had long watched the proceedings of his rival, and every night mounted guard near Camara's tent. At the moment the lovers escaped, he was making his circuit; but immediately perceiving them, he galloped in pursuit. Fehrab's mare, endowed by nature with all the fleetness of the Nedgdian race, and stimulated to greater exertions by her master's impatience, urged her course to its highest speed; but, pressed by a double burden, she could at length no longer give her wonted aid to her master—she fell; and Fehrab, seeing himself on the point of being overtaken by Tamer, lifted his beloved from the horse, and prepared for her defence. The combat was terrible, and its sequel tragical. Tamer was victor, slew Fehrab, and seized his cousin; but, exhausted by fatigue, and now in full security, he fell asleep for a moment by her side. Camara, who had watched the influence of slumber stealing over his senses, snatched up his sabre, stained with the blood of her lover, and cut off the head of her ravisher; then precipitating herself upon the point of his lance, pierced her own heart. The three dead bodies alone were found by those who went in search of them.

A murderous war between the two tribes was the consequence of this melancholy event;— that of Fehrab, supported by the Wahabees, forced Beny Tay to a retreat; and the latter, with four other tribes,* its allies, came to solicit protection from the Drayhy, whose power was henceforth unrivalled. Five hundred thousand Bedouins, allied in our cause, formed but one camp, and overspread Mesopotamia like a cloud of locusts.

While we remained in the neighbourhood of Bagdad, our allies pillaged another caravan coming from Aleppo, laden with productions of European manufacture; cloths, velvets, satins,

* The tribe of Beny Tay, composed of 4,000 tents; that of El Hamarnid, 1,500 tents; of El Daffir, 2,500 tents; of El Hegiager, 800 tents; and lastly, that of El Khresahel, 3,000.

amber, coral, &c.; and although the Drayhy took no part in these spoliations, he was too well versed in Bedouin habits to think of offering any opposition. The Pacha of Bagdad demanded satisfaction, but obtained none; and perceiving that to enforce justice would require an army of at least fifteen thousand men, he renounced his claim, happy to continue in friendship with the Bedouins at any sacrifice.

Sheik Ibrahim now saw his hopes realized beyond even his most sanguine anticipations; but as long as any thing remained to be done, he would allow himself no repose: crossing the Tigris, therefore, at Abou el Ali, we continued our march, and entered Persia. Here, also, the reputation of the Drayhy had preceded him, and the tribes of the country came continually to fraternize with us; but in our vast plan of operations, these partial alliances were insignificant,—we required the co-operation of the great prince, chief of all the Persian tribes, the Emir Sahid el Bokhrani, whose command extends to the frontiers of India. The family of this prince has for many years reigned over the errant tribes of Persia, and claims its descent from the kings Beni el Abass, who conquered Spain, and whose descendants still call themselves the Bokhrani. We learned that he was in a very distant province. The Drayhy having convoked all the chiefs to a general council, it was decided to traverse Persia, keeping as near as possible to the sea-coast, notwithstanding the probable scarcity of water, in order to avoid the mountains which intersect the interior of this country, and to find pasturage. In the itinerary of a tribe, a plentiful supply of grass is more important than water: the latter may be transported, but nothing can remedy a deficiency of food for the cattle, on which the very existence of the tribe itself depends.

This march occupied fifty-one days. During the whole time we encountered no obstacle on the part of the inhabitants, but were often seriously incommoded by the scarcity of water. On one of these occasions, Sheik Ibrahim, having observed the nature of the soil and the freshness of the grass, advised the Drayhy to dig for water. The Bedouins of the country treated the attempt as madness, saying that no water had ever been known in those parts, and that it was necessary to send for it to a distance of six hours. But the Drayhy persevered: "Sheik Ibrahim is a prophet," said he, "and must be obeyed."

Holes were accordingly dug in several places, and at the depth of four feet excellent water was found. Seeing this happy result, the Bedouins by acclamation proclaimed Sheik Ibrahim a true prophet, his discovery a miracle, and, in the excess of their gratitude, had well nigh adored him as a god.

After journeying several days among the mountains and valleys of the Karman, we reached the deep and rapid river Karassan; and having crossed it, proceeded in the direction of the coast, where the road was less difficult. We made acquaintance with the Bedouins of the Agiam Estan, who received us in a very friendly manner; and on the forty-second day after entering

Persia, we arrived at El Hendouan, where one of their greatest tribes was encamped, commanded by Hebiek el Mahdan. We hoped that our long pilgrimage was drawing towards its close; but the sheik informed us that we were still distant nine long days' journeys from Merah Fames, the present residence of the Emir Sahid, on the frontiers of India. He offered us guides to conduct us thither, and described the points where it would be necessary to lay in a provision of water; without which information, we should have been exposed to great danger in this last expedition.

We despatched couriers before us, to give notice to the grand prince of our approach, and of our pacific intentions. On the ninth day he came to meet us, at the head of a formidable army. It did not at first appear very clear whether this demonstration of strength was to do us honour or to intimidate us. The Drayhy began to repent of having ventured so far from his allies. However, he showed no symptom of fear, but placing the women and the baggage behind the troops, he advanced with the choicest of his cavalry, accompanied by his friend the Sheik Saker,—the same to whom in the preceding year he had delegated the command of the desert of Bassora, and who had negotiated all our alliances there during our stay in Syria.

The prince soon satisfied them respecting his intentions; for, detaching himself from this numerous host, he advanced with a small train of horsemen to the middle of the plain which separated the two armies; the Drayhy did the same;

and the two chiefs, on meeting, alighted and embraced with every expression of cordiality.

If I had not so frequently described the hospitality of the desert, I should have much to say on the reception we experienced from the Emir Sahid, and the three days' festivities with which he welcomed us: but, to avoid repetitions, I shall pass over this scene, only remarking, that the Bedouins of Persia, more pacific than those of Arabia, entered readily into our views, and fully understood the importance of the commercial intercourse we were desirous of establishing with India. This was all that it was needful to explain to them of the nature of our enterprise. The emir promised us the co-operation of all the tribes of Persia under his dominion, and offered his influence with those of India, who hold him in high consideration, on account of the antiquity of his race, and of his personal reputation for wisdom and generosity. He entered into a distinct treaty with us, which was drawn up in the following terms:—

"In the name of the clement and merciful God, I, Sahid, son of Bader, son of Abdallah, son of Barakat, son of Ali, son of Bokhrani, of blessed memory: I hereby make a declaration of having given my sacred word to the powerful Drayhy Ebn Chahllan, to Sheik Ibrahim, and to Abdallah el Katib. I declare myself their faithful ally; I accept all the conditions which are specified in the general treaty now in their hands. I engage to assist and support them in all their projects, and to keep their secrets inviolably. Their enemies shall be my enemies; their friends, my friends. I invoke the great Ali, the first of men, and the well-beloved of God, to bear witness to my word.

"Health."

(Signed and sealed.)

We remained six days encamped with the tribe of Sahid, and had thus an opportunity of observing the difference between the customs of these Bedouins and those of our provinces. The Persians are milder, more sober, and more patient; but less brave, less generous, and less respectful to the women: they have more religious prejudices, and follow the precepts of the sect of Ali. Besides the lance, the gun, and the sabre, they use the battle-axe.

Prince Sahid sent to the Drayhy two beautiful Persian mares, led by two negroes: the latter, in return, made him a present of a black mare of great value, of the race of Nedgdie, named Houban Neggir, and added some ornaments for his wives.

We were encamped not far from Menouna, the last town of Persia, twenty leagues from the frontiers of India, on the banks of a river which the Bedouins call El Gitan.

On the seventh day we took leave of Sahid, and recommenced our march, in order to reach Syria again before the heats of summer set in. We marched rapidly, and without precautions, till one day, while we were passing through the province of Karman, our beasts were carried off; and the next day we were ourselves attacked by a powerful tribe, commanded by the Emir Redaini, an imperious man, and jealous of his authority, who constitutes himself the guardian of the caliphate of Persia. These Bedouins, very superior in number, were as much our inferiors in courage and tactics: our troops were vastly better commanded. Our position was, however, extremely critical—we were lost if the enemy gained the smallest advantage; for all the Bedouins of the Karman would at once have surrounded us, and hemmed us in as with a net, from which there would have been no possibility of escaping. The necessity, then, of inspiring them with respect by a decisive victory, which should at once cure them of any inclination to try their strength with us for the future, was imperative; and the Drayhy made the most skilful and best combined dispositions for ensuring the triumph of courage over numbers: he displayed all the resources of his military genius and long experience, and himself performed prodigies of valour,—he had never commanded more calmly, nor fought more impetuously: accordingly, the enemy was obliged to retreat, leaving us at full liberty to pursue our homeward journey. The Drayhy, however, considering that it would not be prudent to leave behind him a hostile though beaten tribe, slackened his march, and sent a courier to the Emir Sahid, to give him intelligence of what had passed. The messenger returned in a few days, bringing a very friendly letter to the Drayhy, enclosing a second, addressed in the following terms to Redaini:

"In the name of God the supreme: Be homage and respectful prayers ever addressed to the greatest, the most powerful, the most honorable, the wisest, and the handsomest of prophets!

the bravest of the brave, the greatest of the great, the caliph of caliphs, the master of the sabre and of the red ruby, the converter of souls, the Iman Ali. This letter is from Sahid el Bokhrani, the grandee of the two seas and of the two Persias, to his brother the Emir Redaini, the son of Kronkiar. We give you to know that our brother the Emir Drayhy Ebn Chahllan, of the country of Bagdad and Damascus, is come from far to visit us and form an alliance with us. He has marched on our land and eaten of our bread; we have granted him our friendship, and moreover have entered into particular engagements with him, from which great good and general tranquillity will result. We desire that you do the same: take care that you do not fail in this point, or you will lose our esteem, and act in opposition to the will of God, and of the glorious Iman Ali."

Here followed many citations from their holy books, the Giaffer el Giameh, and the customary salutations.

We sent this letter to the Emir Redaini, who thereupon came to us, accompanied by five hundred horsemen, all richly dressed in gold brocades: their arms were mounted in chased silver, and the Damascus blades of their sabres exquisitely worked. Some amicable explanations having passed, Redaini copied with his own hand the particular treaty of the Emir Sahid, and signed it: he then took coffee, but refused to dine with us, the fanatics of the sect of Ali being prohibited from eating either with Christians or Turks. To ratify his contract, however, he swore upon bread and salt, and then embraced the Drayhy with great protestations of fraternity. His tribe, called El Mehaziz, numbers ten thousand tents. After taking leave of him, we continued our journey by forced marches, advancing fifteen leagues a day without halting. On reaching Bagdad, Sheik Ibrahim went into the city to take up money; but the season requiring expedition, we lost as little time as possible. In Mesopotamia we got news of the Wahabees. Ebn Sihoud had given a very ill reception to his general, Hedal, after his defeat, and had sworn to send a more powerful army than the former, under his son, to take vengeance upon the Drayhy, and exterminate the Bedouins of Syria; but after having obtained more correct information respecting the resources and personal reputation of the Drayhy, he changed his tone, and resolved to make an effort towards concluding an alliance with him. Foreign events also gave an air of probability to these rumours; for the Pacha of Egypt, Mehemet Ali, was preparing an expedition to invade Arabia Petrea, and to take possession of the riches of Mecca, which, for the present, were in the hands of Ebn Sihoud. Either of these prospects was agreeable to our projects, which would have been equally forwarded, whether his proposed alliance took effect, or whether he was weakened by a foreign power. We were continually meeting on our route tribes which had not yet signed the treaty, but which eagerly took advantage of the opportunity of doing so.*

* At Maktal El Abed, we met two tribes, that of Berkaje, commanded by Sahdoun Ebn Wuali, 1300 tents strong, and that of Mahimen, commanded by Fahed Ebn Salche, of 300

On arriving in Syria, we received a courier from the King of the Wahabees, who brought us a little bit of paper, about three fingers in breadth, and twice as long. They affect to use these diminutive missives in contrast to the Turks, who write their firmans upon large sheets of paper. The Arabian character takes so little room, that in this small space was written a very long and sufficiently imperious letter. It commenced with a sort of confession of faith, or declaration, that God is one, universal, and without equal; then came all the titles of the king whom God has invested with his sabre to maintain his unity against the idolaters (the Christians) who affirm the contrary. And it continued thus:—

"We, Abdallah, son of Abdel Aziz, son of Abdel Wahabs, son of Sihoud: We give you to know, O son of Chahllan, (may the only adorable God direct you in the right way!) that if you believe in God, you must obey his slave Abdallah, to whom he has delegated his power, and come and see us without fear. You shall be our well-beloved son; we will pardon the past, and treat you as one of ourselves. But beware of obstinacy and resistance to our call; for he who listens to us is reckoned in the number of the inhabitants of paradise.

"Health.

"Signed,
"El Manhoud Menalla Ebn Sihoud Abdallah."

tents. Crossing the Euphrates before Haiff, we concluded an alliance with Alayan Ebn Nadjed, chief of the tribe of Bouharba, which reckoned 500 tents.

On the reception of this letter we held a great council of war; and after having deliberately weighed all the perils of the journey against the advantages of the alliance of Ebn Sihoud, the Drayhy determined to comply with this authoritative invitation. Sheik Ibrahim having asked me if I felt my courage equal to undertaking a visit to this fanatic, I replied:

"I am well aware that my risk is greater than that of others, on account of his hatred of all Christians; but I put my confidence in God. I must die once, and having already made a sacrifice of my life, I am willing to undertake any task likely to promote the entire execution of the enterprise upon which I have entered."

A desire of seeing this extraordinary man and his curious country also excited my courage, and having earnestly recommended my poor mother to the protection of M. Lascaris, if I should die in this expedition, I set out with the Drayhy, his second son Sahdoun, his nephew, his cousin, two of the principal chiefs, and five negroes, all mounted on dromedaries. During his father's absence, Saher was to command the tribe, and conduct it to Horran, to meet the Drayhy, who proposed returning by the Hegiaz. We made our first halt among the Bedouins Beny Toulab, whose sole wealth consists in a few asses, and who live by hunting gazelles and ostriches. They wear the skins of gazelles coarsely sewed together, forming long robes with very large sleeves; and the fur being outside, their appearance much resembles that of wild beasts: I have never seen anything so savage as their aspect. They showed us an ostrich hunt, in which I was greatly interested. The female ostrich lays her eggs in the sand, and takes up her station at some distance, looking fixedly upon them: she covers them as it were, with her eyes, which she never turns from the nest. She remains thus immovable for half the day, until the male comes to relieve her. She then goes in search of food whilst her mate keeps guard in his turn. The hunter, when he has discovered the eggs, constructs a sort of shed with stones to conceal himself, and waits behind it for the favourable moment. When the female is left alone, and the male at a sufficient distance to prevent his taking alarm at the report, he draws his trigger, runs to pick up the unfortunate bird who has received her mortal wound, wipes away the blood, and replaces her in her former position near the eggs; the male, on his return, approaches fearlessly to assume his office of guard, when the hunter, who has remained in ambuscade, shoots him also, and thus bears away a double prize. If the male has had any cause of alarm, he runs with velocity to a distance; and if pursued, defends himself by flinging stones behind him with extraordinary force, to the extent of a musket-shot:—it is moreover prudent to keep at a distance from him when in a state of irritation, for his elevated stature and vigorous strength would render a close encounter very perilous, especially to the hunter's eyes. When the season of the ostrich chase is over, the Bedouins carry the feathers to Damascus, or even as far as Bagdad, for sale.

These hunters, when about to marry, pledge half the profits of the ensuing year's chase to the father of the intended bride, as her dowry. They hold the memory of Antar in high veneration, and proclaim themselves his descendants: but how far the pretension is admissible, I know not. They recite, however, numerous fragments of his poem.

After taking leave of them, we still proceeded at the rapid pace of our dromedaries, and encamped on the borders of a very extensive lake, called Raam Beni Hellal, which receives its waters from a mountain which we had skirted.

The next day, having reached the middle of a dry and barren desert, we discovered a little oasis, formed by the shrub called jorfa, and had arrived within a few paces of it, when our dromedaries suddenly stopped short, which we at first attributed to their inclination for resting in a spot where the appearance of vegetation announced the probable presence of water: but it was soon evident that their repugnance arose from instinctive terror, manifested by all its outward tokens: neither caresses nor menaces could induce them to stir. My curiosity being excited to the highest degree, I alighted to investigate the cause of their alarm: but I had no sooner entered the thicket, than I involuntarily recoiled, for the ground was strewed with the skins of serpents of all sizes and species. There were thousands of them; some of the thickness of a ship's cable, others as small as needles. We hurried from the spot, offering up thanksgivings to God that the skins alone of these venomous reptiles had fallen in our way. No shelter appearing as night closed in, we were obliged to pass it in the open desert: but the horrible spectacle of the thicket was too forcibly impressed upon my imagination to permit me to close my eyes; I expected every moment to see an enormous serpent glide under the covering of my tent, and rear its menacing head beside my pillow.

The following day we overtook a considerable tribe of Wahabees coming from Samarcand: we carefully concealed our pipes from them,—for Ebn Sihoud severely prohibits smoking, and punishes any infraction of his laws with death. The Emir Medjioun hospitably entertained us, but could not suppress his surprise at our hardihood in thus placing ourselves at the mercy of the Wahabee, whose ferocious character he depicted to us in the most frightful terms. He did not dissemble that we ran great hazard; Ebn Sihoud's deceitful promises, which he lavishes without scruple, being no guarantee against the most infamous treachery. The Drayhy himself, full of loyalty, had advanced on the faith of the king's invitation, his imagination never suggesting the possibility of a breach of promise, and began now to repent his too credulous confidence; but pride prevented his retreating, and we prosecuted our journey. We soon reached the Nedgde, a country intersected with mountains and valleys, studded with nomade camps, and abounding in towns and villages, the former of which appear to be very ancient, and attest a former population much richer and more numerous than that by which they are now occupied. The villages are peopled with Bedouin husbandmen; and the soil produces corn, table vegeta-

bles, and dates in abundance. We were told by
the inhabitants, that the aborigines had abandoned their country to establish themselves in Africa,
under the conduct of one of their princes, named
Beni Hetal.

We everywhere experienced a warm-hearted
hospitality, but heard interminable complaints of
the tyranny of Ebn Sihoud, under whose dominion these people seem to be retained by fear
alone.

At length after fourteen days' journey, at the
pace of our dromedaries, which may be reckoned
at triple the distance traversed by a caravan in
the same space of time, we arrived in the capital
of the Wahabees. The city is surrounded and
concealed by a wood of palms, called the Palm-
trees of Darkisch, which serves it as a rampart,
and is so thickly planted as scarcely to admit the
passage of a horseman between the trunks of the
trees. Having made our way through these, we
came to a second barrier, composed of little hil-
locks of date-stones, resembling a bank of small
pebbles, and behind it the town-wall, along
which we rode to the entrance-gate, and, passing
through it, soon reached the king's palace, a
large edifice of two stories, built of white hewn
stones.

Ebn Sihoud, on being informed of our arrival,
ordered us to be ushered into an elegant and
well-furnished apartment, where a plentiful repast was set before us. This beginning seemed
to. augur well, and we congratulated ourselves
upon not having yielded to the suspicions which
had been suggested to us. The same night, having suitably attired ourselves, we were presented

to the king; whom we found to be about forty-five years of age, with a harsh countenance, a bronzed complexion, and a very black beard. He was dressed in a robe fastened round the loins by a white sash, a striped turban of red and white on his head, and a black embroidered mantle thrown over his left shoulder, holding in his right hand the sceptre of the King of Mahlab, the ensign of his authority. He was seated, surrounded by the grandees of his court, at the extremity of a large audience-chamber, richly furnished with mats, carpets, and cushions. The draperies, as well as the king's habiliments, were of cotton or the wool of Yemen,—silk being prohibited in his dominions, together with everything that would recall the luxury or customs of the Turks. I had leisure for making my observations; for when Ebn Sihoud had answered concisely and in a chilling tone to the Drayhy's compliments, we seated ourselves, and waited in silence till he should propose a subject of conversation. The Drayhy, however, observing that after half an hour had elapsed he neither ordered coffee nor cleared his brow, opened the conference himself by thus addressing him:—

"I see, O son of Sihoud, that our reception from you is not such as we had a right to expect. We have travelled through your territories, and are come under your roof, upon your own invitation: if you have anything to allege against us, speak—conceal nothing from us."

Ebn Sihoud, casting a fiery glance at him, replied:

"Yes, truly, I have many things to allege against you: your crimes are unpardonable!

You have revolted against me; you have refused to obey me, and you have devastated the tribe of Sachrer, in Galilee, knowing that it belonged to me.

" You have corrupted the Bedouins, and confederated them against me, and against my authority.

" You have destroyed my armies, pillaged my camps, and supported my mortal enemies, those idolaters, those profaners, those rascals, those debauchees, the Turks."

Growing more and more exasperated as he spoke, and accumulating invective upon invective, his rage at last exceeded all bounds, and he concluded by commanding us to leave his presence and await his pleasure.

I saw the Drayhy's eyes kindle, his nostrils swell, and I dreaded every instant an explosion of impotent wrath, which could only have served to drive the king to extremities; but, reflecting that he was entirely defenceless, he refrained himself, rose with dignity, and slowly retired to meditate what course he should pursue. All men trembled before the fury of Ebn Sihoud, and none dared to oppose his will. For two days and nights we remained in our apartment, hearing and seeing nothing. No one cared to approach us; even those who on our first arrival appeared most forward in our service, either shunned us, or laughed at our easy credulity in the good faith of a man whose perfidious and sanguinary character was so well known. We expected momentarily to see the tyrant's satellites appear to massacre us, and sought in vain for some means of extricating ourselves from his grasp. On the third day, the Drayhy, declaring he preferred death to suspense, sent for one of the ministers of the Wahabee, named Abou el Sallem, and commissioned him to deliver this message to his master.

"What you propose to do, do quickly; I shall not reproach you—I shall blame myself alone for surrendering myself into your hands."

El Sallem obeyed, but returned not; and our only answer was the sight of twenty-five armed negroes, who ranged themselves before our door. We were then decidedly prisoners!—how I deprecated the foolish curiosity which had so gratuitously drawn me into peril! The Drayhy had no fear of death; but constraint was insupportable to him,—he walked to and fro with rapid strides, like a lion before the bars of his cage, and at last broke out :—

"I am determined to make an end of the matter; I will speak to Ebn Sihoud and reproach him with his perfidy; I see that mildness and patience are unavailing, and I am resolved to die with dignity."

Again he summoned El Sallem; and the moment he appeared, "Return to your master, said he, "and inform him that by the faith of the Bedouins I demand the right of speaking to him: there will still be time to follow his own pleasure after he has heard me."

The Wahabee granted an audience, and El Sallem introduced us. Arrived in his presence, the king left us standing, and made no return to our customary salutations.

"What do you want?" said he roughly.

The Drayhy, drawing himself up with dignity, replied:

"I am come to see you, O son of Sihoud, on the faith of your promises, and with a suite of only ten men: I command thousands of warriors. We are defenceless in your hands, you are in the centre of your power:—you may crush us like ashes; but know, that from the frontier of India, to the frontier of Nedgde, in Persia, in Bussora, in Mesopotamia, Hemad, the two Syrias, Galilee, and Horan, every man who wears the caftan will demand my blood at your hands, and will take vengeance for my death. If you are, as you pretend, the King of the Bedouins, how can you stoop to treachery? that is the vile practice of the Turks. Treachery is not for the strong, but for the weak or the cowardly. You who boast of your armies, and claim to hold your authority from God himself, if you would not tarnish your glory, restore me to my country, and openly contend with me by force of arms; for, by abusing my confidence, you will dishonour yourself, render yourself an object of universal contempt, and occasion the ruin of your kingdom. I have said: now take your pleasure,—but you will one day repent it. I am only one among thousands: my death will not diminish my tribe, will not extinguish the race of Cholan. My son Sahen will supply my place: he remains to lead my Bedouins, and to avenge my blood. Be warned then, and open your eyes to the truth."

During this harangue, the king stroked his beard, and gradually calmed himself. After a moment's silence:

"Go in peace," said he; "nothing but good will happen to you."

We then retired, but were still guarded.

This successful beginning encouraged the courtiers, who had heard with terror the daring words of the Drayhy, and were astonished at the tyrant's endurance of them. They began again to gather round us, and Abou el Sallem invited us to dinner. But I did not feel very confident on my own score; I thought indeed Ebn Sihoud might not venture upon extremities with the Drayhy, but feared lest he might ascribe his wrongs to my counsels, and sacrifice me, an obscure giaour, to his resentment. These apprehensions I imparted to the Drayhy, who reassured me, swearing that no attempt should reach me but over his corpse, and that I should first pass out through the gates of Darkisch.

The next day Ebn Sihoud sent for us, received us very graciously, and had coffee served to us. Presently he began to question the Drayhy about the persons who accompanied him. My turn is now coming, thought I, and my heart palpitated a little. I recovered myself, however; and when the Drayhy had named me, the king, turning towards me, said:

"You then are Abdallah the Christian?"

And on my answering in the affirmative,

"I see," continued he, "that your actions are much greater than your stature."

"A musket-ball," I replied, "is small, yet it kills great men."

He smiled.

"I find it very difficult," he resumed, "to credit all that I hear of you: I would have you answer me frankly; what is the object of the alliance which you have been labouring so many years to accomplish?"

" Its object is very simple," answered I. "We are desirous to unite all the Bedouins of Syria under the command of the Drayhy, to resist the Turks; you may perceive that we are by these means forming an impenetrable barrier between you and your enemies."

" Very well," said he; " but that being your object, why did you endeavour to destroy my armies before Hama?"

" Because," I replied, " you were an obstacle to our projects. It was not for you, but for the Drayhy, that we were labouring. His power once established in Syria, Mesopotamia, and to the confines of Persia, we were willing to enter into alliance with you, and become by that means invulnerable in the possession of our entire liberty. Children of the same nation, we have but one cause to defend: for this purpose we came here to cement an indissoluble union with you. You received us in an offensive manner, and the Drayhy on his part has reproached you in offensive terms; but our intentions were sincere, and we have proved them so by confiding ourselves unarmed to your good faith."

The king's countenance cleared up more and more as I spoke; and when I had ceased, he said,

" I am satisfied."

Then, turning to his slaves, he ordered *three* cups of coffee. I internally thanked God for inspiring me with words that proved so successful. The rest of the visit passed off well, and we retired well satisfied. In the evening we were invited by one of the ministers to a grand supper, and confidentially entertained with the cruelties of his master, and the universal execration in which he was held. His immense treasures were also a topic of discussion: those he had acquired by the pillage of Mecca are incalculable. From the earliest period of the Hegira, Mussulman princes, the caliphs, the sultans, and the kings of Persia, send annually to the tomb of the Prophet considerable presents in jewels, lamps, and candelabras of gold, precious stones, &c. besides the offerings from the commonalty of the faithful. The throne alone, the gift of a Persian king, composed of massive gold, inlaid with pearls and diamonds, was of inestimable value. Every prince on his accession sends a crown of gold, enriched with precious stones, to be suspended from the roofs of the chapel, and they were innumerable when Ebn Sihoud plundered it: one diamond alone, as large as a walnut, was considered invaluable. When we consider all that the lapse of centuries had accumulated on that one point, it is not surprising that the king should have carried away forty camels laden with jewellery, besides articles of massive gold and silver. Taking into calculation these inexhaustible treasures, and the tithes which he raises annually from his allies, I think he may be regarded as the richest monarch upon earth; especially as his expenses are very trifling,—as he rigorously prohibits luxury, and as in time of war each tribe furnishes subsistence for its armies, and bears all its own charges and losses, for which no compensation is ever recovered.

So delighted was I with the recovery of my

liberty, that I spent all the next day in walking about and visiting every part of Darkisch and its environs. The town, built of white stone, contains seven thousand inhabitants, almost all kinsmen, ministers, or generals of Ebn Sihoud. No artizans are found there. The only trades exercised in the town are those of armourers and farriers, and few persons are engaged even in them. Nothing is to be purchased, not even food, for which every one depends on his own means,—that is to say, upon an estate or garden, producing corn, vegetables and fruits, and affording nourishment to a few fowls. Their numerous herds browse in the plain; and every Wednesday the inhabitants of Yemen and Mecca assemble to exchange their merchandise for cattle; a species of fair, which forms the sole commerce of the country. The women appear unveiled, but throw their black mantles over their faces,—a very disgraceful custom: they are generally ugly and excessively dark-complexioned. The gardens, situated in a charming valley near the town, on the opposite side to that by which we had entered, produce the finest fruits in the world,—bananas, oranges, pomegranates, figs, apples, melons, &c. intermixed with barley and maize,—and are carefully watered.

The next morning, the king again summoned us to him, received us very graciously, and questioned me closely respecting the various European sovereigns, especially Napoleon, for whom he testified great admiration. Nothing delighted him so much as the recital of the emperor's conquests; and happily my frequent intercourse with M. Lascaris had furnished me with many details to entertain him with. At the account of every battle, he would exclaim—

"Surely this man is an emissary of God : I am persuaded he must be in intimate communion with his Creator, since he is thus singularly favoured."

His affability towards me having gradually but rapidly increased, he suddenly changed the subject of conversation, and said at last,

"Abdallah, I desire to hear the truth from you: what is the basis of Christianity ?"

Aware of the Wahabee's prejudices, I trembled at this question; but mentally praying for divine inspiration,

"The basis of all religion, O son of Sihoud!" I said, "is belief in God. The Christians deem, as you do, that there is one only God, the Creator of the universe; who punishes the wicked, pardons the penitent, and recompenses the good : that He alone is great, merciful, and almighty."

"Very well," said he; "but how do you pray ?"

I repeated the *Pater-noster* : he made his secretary write at my dictation, read and re-read it, and placed it inside his vest; then, pursuing his interrogatory, asked me to which side we turned to pray.

"We pray on all sides," answered I, "for God is everywhere."

"That opinion I entirely approve," said he: "but you must have precepts as well as prayers."

I repeated the ten commandments given by God to his prophet Moses, which he appeared to know, and continued his inquiries.

"And Jesus Christ,—in what light do you consider him?"

"As the Incarnate Word of God."

"But he was crucified?"

"As the Divine Word, he could not die; but as man, he suffered for the sins of the wicked."

"That is marvellous. And the sacred book which God inspired through Jesus Christ, is it revered among you?—do you exactly conform to its doctrine?"

"We preserve it with the greatest reverence, and in all things obey its injunctions."

"The Turks," said he, "have made a god of their prophet, and pray over his tomb like idolaters. Cursed be those who ascribe to the Creator an equal! may the sabre exterminate them!"

His invectives against the Turks increasing in vehemence, he proceeded to censure the use of the pipe, of wine, and of unclean meats; while I was too happy in having adroitly extricated myself from the discussion of dangerous questions, to presume to contradict him on insignificant points, and allowed him to believe me a despiser of that villanous herb, as he called tobacco; which drew a smile from the Drayhy, who was well aware that the present prohibition of it was the greatest possible privation to me, and that I availed myself of every opportunity which promised impunity to withdraw my beloved pipe from its concealment: that day, in particular, my longing for it was extreme, having talked much and drunk very strong Mocha coffee.

The king appeared delighted with our conversation, and said to me,—"I see that we may always learn something. I have hitherto believed the Christians to be the most superstitious of men; but I am now convinced that they approach much nearer to the true religion than the Turks."

Ebn Sihoud is on the whole a well-informed and very eloquent man, but fanatical in his religious opinions: he has a legitimate wife and a concubine; two sons, both married, and a daughter still young. He eats nothing but what is prepared by his wives, for fear of being poisoned. The guard of his palace is committed to a troop of a thousand well-armed negroes. He can raise within his territories fifteen hundred thousand Bedouins capable of bearing arms. When he intends to nominate the governor of a province, he invites the person on whom his choice has fallen to dinner, and after the repast they unite in ablutions and prayer; after which the king, arming him with a sabre, says to him,—

"I have elected you, by command of God, to govern these slaves: be humane and just; gather punctually the tithe, and cut off the heads of Turks and infidels who say that God has an equal—let none such establish themselves within your jurisdiction. May the Lord give victory to those who believe in his unity!"

He then delivers to him a small writing, enjoining the inhabitants to obey the governor in all things, under the severest penalties.

The next day we visited the king's stables; and I think it would be impossible for an amateur of horses to have a more gratifying sight. The first objects of attention were twenty-four white mares, ranged in single file, all of incomparable beauty, and so exactly alike that it was not possible to distinguish the one from the other: their hair, brilliant as silver, dazzled my eyes. A hundred and twenty others, of various coats, but equally elegant in form, occupied another building; and even I, notwithstanding my antipathy to horses since the accident which had so nearly cost my life, could not help admiring the beautiful tenants of these stables.

We supped that evening with Hedal, the general-in-chief, who was reconciled with the Drayhy; and the famous Abou Nocta, who was of the party, was extremely polite to him. For several days we met in secret conclave, treating with Ebn Sihoud; but the details of the negotiation would be superfluous. It is sufficient to say, that an alliance was concluded between him and the Drayhy to their mutual satisfaction, and the king declared *that their two bodies would be henceforth directed by one soul.* The treaty being ratified, he invited us for the first time to eat with him, and tasted each dish before it was offered to us. As he had never seen any one eat otherwise than with their fingers, I carved a spoon and fork out of a piece of wood, spread my handkerchief for a napkin, and ate my dinner after the European fashion, which highly diverted him.

"Thanks be to God!" said he, "every nation believes its customs the best possible, and each is therefore content with its condition."

Our departure being fixed for the following day, the king sent us as a present seven of his most beautiful mares, their bridles held by as many black slaves mounted on camels; and when each of us had made his choice, we were presented with sabres, the blades of which were very handsome, but the scabbards quite unornamented. To our servants also he gave more ordinary sabres, saddle-cloths, and a hundred tallarins each.

We took leave of Ebn Sihoud with the customary ceremonies, and were accompanied beyond the walls by all the officers of his court. Arrived at the gates, the Drayhy stopped, and turning to me, invited me to pass first, wishing, he told me, with a smile, to keep his promise. And I confess, that all the civilities we had latterly received, had not so far effaced from my mind the impression of the suspense and anguish we had previously experienced, but that I rejoiced to find myself beyond the barriers.

We took the road to Heggias, resting every night with one of the tribes which overspread the desert. The fifth day, after passing the night under the tents of El Henadi, we rose with the sun, and went out to saddle our dromedaries; but found them, to our great amazement, with their heads plunged deeply into the sand, from whence it was impossible to disengage them. Calling to our aid the Bedouins of the tribe, they informed us that the circumstance presaged the simoom, which would not long delay its devastating course, and that we could not proceed without facing certain death. Providence has endowed the camel with an instinctive presentiment for its preservation. It is sensible two or three hours beforehand of the approach of this terrific scourge of the desert, and turning its face away from the wind, buries itself in the sand; and neither force nor want can move it from its position, either to eat or drink, while the tempest lasts, though it should be for several days.

Learning the danger which threatened us, we shared the general terror, and hastened to adopt all the precautions enjoined us. Horses must not only be placed under shelter, but have their heads covered and their ears stopped; they would otherwise be suffocated by the whirlwinds of fine and subtle sand which the wind sweeps furiously before it. Men assemble under their tents, stopping up every crevice with extreme caution; and having provided themselves with water placed within reach, throw themselves on the ground, covering their heads with a mantle, and stir no more till the desolating hurricane has passed.

That morning all was tumult in the camp; every one endeavouring to provide for the safety of his beasts, and then precipitately retiring under the protection of his tent. We had scarcely time to secure our beautiful Nedgde mares before the storm began. Furious gusts of wind were succeeded by clouds of red and burning sands, whirling round with fierce impetuosity, and overthrowing or burying under their drifted mountains whatever they encountered. If any part of the body is by accident exposed to its touch, the flesh swells as if a hot iron had been passed over it. The water intended to refresh us with its coolness was boiling, and the temperature of the tent exceeded that of a Turkish bath. The tempest lasted ten hours in its greatest fury, and then gradually sunk for the following six: another hour, and we must all have been suffocated. When at length we ventured to issue from our tents, a dreadful spectacle awaited us: five children, two women, and a man were extended dead on the still burning sand; and several Bedouins had their faces blackened and entirely calcined, as if by the action of an ardent furnace. When any one is struck on the head by the simoom, the blood flows in torrents from his mouth and nostrils, his face swells and turns black, and he soon dies of suffocation. We thanked the Lord that we had not ourselves been surprised by this terrible scourge in the midst of the desert, but had been preserved from so frightful a death.

When the weather permitted us to leave the camp of Henadi, twelve hours' march brought us back to our tribe. I embraced Sheik Ibrahim with true filial love, and several days elapsed in the mutual recital of our adventures. When I had perfectly recovered my fatigues, M. Lascaris said to me:

"My dear son, we have no longer any business here. Thanks be to God, all is accomplished! and my enterprise has succeeded beyond my most sanguine hopes: we must now return to give an account of our mission."

We quitted our friends in the hope of soon seeing them at the head of the expedition to which we had opened and smoothed the way. Passing through Damascus, Aleppo, and Caramania, we reached Constantinople in the month of April, after ninety days' travelling, frequently across tracts of snow. In the course of that fatiguing journey I lost my handsome Nedgdian mare, the gift of Ebn Sihoud, which I had calculated on selling for at least thirty thousand piastres: but this was only the forerunner of the misfortunes which awaited us. Constantinople was ravaged by the plague; and General Andreossi lodged us at Keghat-Kani, where we spent three months in quarantine, and, during that time, were informed of the fatal catastrophe of Moscow and the retreat of the French army upon Paris. M. Lascaris was in despair, and for two months his plan of proceeding was quite undecided. At length, determining to return into Syria, and there wait the issue of events, we embarked on board a vessel freighted with corn; but a violent storm drove us to Chios, where we again encountered the plague. M. de Bourville, the French consul, procured us a lodging, in which we remained for two months closely shut up; and there, our property having become a prey to the tempest, while contagion cut us off from all external communication, we were nearly without clothing, and exposed to the greatest privations.

Communications were at length restored; and M. Lascaris having received a letter from our consul-general at Smyrna, inviting him to a conference there with the Generals Lallemand and Savary, determined to comply, and allowed me meanwhile to visit my poor mother, whom I had not seen for six years.

My travels no longer offering any thing of interest to the public, I shall pass over the interval which elapsed between my separation from M. Lascaris and my return to Syria, and hasten to the melancholy conclusion.

While staying at Latakia with my mother, and daily expecting the arrival of a ship that might transport me to Egypt, where I had been ordered by M. Lascaris to rejoin him, I saw a French brig of war enter the port, and hastened to inquire for letters. Alas! those letters brought me the afflicting intelligence of the decease of my benefactor at Cairo. My grief baffled description: I entertained a filial affection for M. Lascaris; besides which, all my future prospects had expired with him. M. Drovetti, French consul in Alexandria, wrote to desire I would come to him as soon as possible; but it was forty days before I could find an opportunity of embarking, and when I reached Alexandria, M. Drovetti had set out for Upper Egypt; thither I followed, and overtook him at Asscout. He informed me that M. Lascaris having entered Egypt with an English passport, Mr. Salt, the English consul, had taken possession of all his effects. He persuaded me, therefore, to apply to that gentleman for payment of my stipend of five hundred tallarins per annum, which was nearly six years in arrear; and especially recommended me to insist strongly on the restitution of M. Lascaris's manuscript journal, a document of vast importance.

I immediately returned to Cairo; but Mr. Salt received me very coldly, and told me that M. Lascaris having died under English protection, he had transmitted his property and papers to England. All my attempts were therefore futile; and after a long detention at Cairo, in the vain hope of obtaining either payment of my arrears or the papers of my patron, Mr. Salt at last menaced me with procuring my arrest by the Egyptian authorities; and to the protection of M. Drovetti alone I owe my escape from this new peril. Weary of so profitless a struggle, I returned to Latakia and my family, more unhappy and less rich than I had at first quitted it on my expedition to Aleppo.

END OF FATALLA SAYEGHIR'S STORY.

NOTE.

It was my intention to have added here a few translations, for the purpose of giving the reader some idea of modern Arabian poetry; but I understand that an able hand, and one more practised than mine, is already employed on the task. A volume, entitled *A Miscellany of French and Oriental Literature*, by J. Augoub, will appear in a few days.* I was acquainted with the author, a young poet of the highest promise, prematurely snatched from his family and his fame. He was born in Egypt, and had been educated in France. The original fragments which he has left behind, and doubtless also these translations, breathe the deep and ardent colouring of his native skies, combined with the purity of French taste. These works, published by his widow, are the only legacy he has bequeathed to his family and his country.

I have inserted in these volumes a few fragments extracted from the publication here announced, assured that they will but stimulate the reader's desire for a further acquaintance with them. A. DE LAMARTINE.

15th April, 1835.

* Published by Abel Ledoux.

MAOULS,

Or Popular Romances of the Modern Arabs; extracted from a Collection entitled, "A Miscellany of French and Oriental Literature," by *J. Augoub.*

Now that thy stature, like the young shoot of a palm, is slender and graceful, grant me thy caresses. O my best beloved, let us make use of time as it flies! Close not against love the avenue to thy favour. Believe me, beauty is evanescent; its empire has never yet been prolonged for a mortal.

They have compared thee to the queen of the nightly firmament; but how greatly do they err in their language! Has the moon those beautiful black eyes, with their sparkling pupils? The rushes bend and sway before the gentlest breath of the zephyr; thou, who resemblest them by thy slight figure—thou seest all men bend before thee!

If the torment of my heart causes happiness to thine, torment me; for my happiness is bound up in thine,—if, indeed, thine is not far dearer to me than my own. If thou wishest to take my life—if the sacrifice of it is necessary to thee—take it, O thou who alone art my life, and incense not thyself against me!

What harm would it be, young beauty, if thou shouldest treat me with more justice? Thou wouldest cure my grievous malady by a remedy which would relieve me from the necessity of having recourse to the Canon of Avicene.* Whenever I contemplate thy beautiful eyebrows, I recognize in them the graceful contour of the houn;† and thy voice is sweeter to my ear than the sound of the harp and the cithern.‡

* The celebrated treatise on medicine by Ebn Sina.
† This Arabic letter is of a bent form. ‡ A stringed instrument.

When my best beloved passed by, the branch of the neighbouring willow was jealous of her delicate figure; the rose bent her head for shame when she saw the bright colour of her cheek; and I exclaimed,—O thou who beyond recovery hast captivated my soul, the glance of thine eye has opened a wound in my bosom which will not be cured to the end of my life!

I love, I love an adolescent, and my passion burns like a flame at the bottom of my heart. When love glided into my bosom, scarcely did the tender down shade the cheek of my lover. Oh, I love! and it is for thee, my well-beloved, that my tears flow; and I swear by Him who created love, that my heart has never known tenderness but for thee! I offer to thee my first flame.

When the night deepens its shadows, it is to imitate the blackness of thy curling locks; when the day shines in its purest splendour, it is to recall to mind the dazzling brightness of thy countenance: the exhalations of the aloes are less sweet than the perfume of thy breath; and the lover, enamoured of thy charms, shall pass his life in recounting thy praises.

My best-beloved comes forth, but her countenance is veiled; yet at sight of her all minds are bewildered. The slender branch in the Valley of Camels becomes jealous of her flexible and attractive form. Suddenly she raises her hand and removes the curious veil which concealed her, and the inhabitants of the land utter cries of surprise. Is it a flash of lightning, say they, which illuminates our dwellings? or have the Arabs lighted fires in the desert?

Names of Tribes.	Names of Commanders of Tribes.	Number of Tents in each Tribe.	Probable Number of Persons in each Tribe.
El-Ammour	Soultan El-Brrak	500	5,000
El-Hassné	Mehamma El Fadel Eben Melhgem	1,500	15,000
Would Aly	Douhi Eben Sammir	5,000	50,000
El-Serhaan	Adgham Eben Ali	1,200	12,000
El-Sarddié	Fedghem Eben Sarraage	1,800	18,000
Benni Sakhrer	Sellamé Eben Fakhrer	2,700	27,000
El-Doualla	Drayhy Eben Chahllan	5,000	50,000
El-Harba	Fares El-Harba	4,000	40,000
El-Suallemè	Auad Eben Giandal	1,500	15,000
El-Ollama	Taffaissan Eben Sarraage	1,400	14,000
Abdellé	Selam Eben Mehgiel	1,200	12,000
El-Refacha	Zarrak	800	8,000
El-Wualdè	Giandal El-Mehidi	1,600	16,000
El-Mofanfakhr	Hammoud El-Tammer	5,000	50,000
El-Cherarah	Abedd Eben Sobaihi	2,300	23,000
El-Achgaha	Dehass Eben Ali	2,000	20,000
El-Salca	Giassem Eben Geraimess	3,000	30,000
El-Giomllan	Zarrak Ebn Fakhrer	1,200	12,000
El-Giahma	Giarah Eben Mehgiel	1,500	15,000
El-Ballahiss	Ghaleb Eben Ramdoun	1,400	14,000
El-Maslekhr	Faress Eben Nadjed	2,000	20,000
El-Khrassa	Zehayran Eben Houad	2,000	20,000
El-Mahlac	Nabec Eben Habed	3,000	30,000
El-Merackhrat	Roudan Eben Soultan	1,500	15,000
El-Zeker	Motlac Eben Fayhan	800	8,000
El-Bechakez	Faress Eben Aggib	500	5,000
El-Chiamssi	Cassem El-Wukban	1,000	10,000
El-Fuaher	Sallamé El-Nahessan	600	6,000
El-Salba	Mehanna El-Saneh	800	8,000
El-Fedhan	Douackhry Eben Ghabiaïn	5,000	50,000
El-Salkeh	Ali Eben Geraimess	3,000	30,000
El-Messahid	Nehaiman Eben Fehed	3,500	35,000
El-Sabha	Mohdi Eben Heïd	4,000	40,000
Benni Dehabb	Chatti Eben Harab	5,000	50,000
El-Fekaka	Astaoui Eben Tayar	1,500	15,000
El-Hamamid	Chatti Eben Faress	15,00	15,000
El-Daffir	Auad Eben Motlac	23,00	23,000
El-Hegiager	Sellamé Eben Barac	800	8,000
El-Khrezahel	Khrenkiar El-Alimy	3,000	30,000
Benni Tay	Hamdi Eben Tamer	4,000	40,000
El-Huarig	Habac Eben Mahdan	3,500	35,000
El-Mehazez	Redaini Eben Khronkiar	6,000	60,000
El-Berkazè	Sahdoun Eben Wuali	1,300	13,000
El-Nahimm	Faheh Eben Saleh	300	3,000
Bouharba	Alyan Eben Nadjed	500	5,000
		102,000	1,020,000

THE END.